GW00361186

Department of Health

Fostering Services

National Minimum Standards

Fostering Services Regulations

London: The Stationery Office

103289283

First published 2002

ISBN 0 11 322540 7

Web Access
This document is available on the DoH internet web site at:
http://www.doh.gov.uk/ncsc

Printed in the United Kingdom for The Stationery Office
ID 89165   716057   03/02   19585

National Minimum Standards for Fostering Services

A statement of national minimum standards published by the Secretary of State for Health under section 23(1) of the Care Standards Act 2000.

March 2002

National Minimum Standards for Fostering Services

Note

This document contains a statement of national minimum standards published by the Secretary of State under section 23(1) of the Care Standards Act 2000. The statement is applicable to fostering agencies as defined by section 4 of that Act.

The statement is accompanied, for explanatory purposes only, by an introduction to the statement as a whole, and a further introduction to each group of standards.

Each individual standard is numbered and consists of the numbered heading and numbered paragraphs. Each standard is, for explanatory purposes only, preceded by a title and where relevant, an indication of the intended outcome in relation to that standard.

Department of Health

Contents

General Introduction

This document contains the fostering services regulations and national minimum standards applicable to fostering services. Together, these regulations and standards form the basis of the new regulatory framework under the Care Standards Act 2000 (CSA) for the conduct of fostering services.

Regulatory Context

The regulations and standards replace The Foster Placement (Children) Regulations 1991. They are applicable to local authority fostering services, independent fostering agencies, and voluntary organisations providing fostering services under s59 of the Children Act 1989.

The regulations are made under sections 22 and 48 of the CSA, which provides the powers for making regulations to govern the conduct of services to be regulated by the National Care Standards Commission (NCSC), and powers under the Children Act 1989 to make regulations about the placing of children with foster parents. The national minimum standards are issued under sections 23 and 49 of the Act.

The CSA establishes the NCSC, an independent, non-governmental public body to regulate social and health care services previously regulated by local councils and health authorities. In addition, the CSA extends the scope of regulation significantly to other services not currently registered, such as independent fostering agencies, and provides for the inspection of local authority fostering services by the NCSC.

How Regulations and Standards work together

The relationship between the regulations and standards and how they operate in practice are very important. The regulations are mandatory and fostering service providers must comply with them. The standards must be taken into account by the NCSC in making its decisions.

Impact on Independent Fostering Agencies and Voluntary Organisations

If a regulation is breached, the breach of which is an offence, providers will be given a notice setting out:

- the regulation breached;
- how the service is considered deficient;
- what must be done to remedy the deficiency; and
- a time scale within which the deficiency must be remedied.

If a deficiency is not remedied, a prosecution may follow. The sequence outlined above illustrates how the process may escalate according to the response of the provider. The standards will be taken into account by the NCSC in its decisions, regarding registration, the imposition of conditions for registration, variation of any conditions, cancellation of registration and enforcement.

Impact on Local Authorities

In the case of local authority fostering services there is an enforcement route via the Secretary of State under the provisions of section 47 of the Act. If there is a substantial failure in meeting the regulations, then the Commission will report them to the Secretary of State for Health, who will take the necessary actions to ensure that the local authority services meet the requirements. If there is a failure, but it is not substantial, the NCSC may serve an enforcement notice under section 47(5) on the local authority. The standards will be taken into account in determining whether the service has met the regulatory requirements.

Role of the Commission

When the Commission makes a decision about a breach of regulations (or any decision to do with registration, cancellation, variation or imposition of conditions) it must take the national minimum standards into account. It may also take into account any other factors it considers reasonable or relevant to do so.

The Commission could decide there has been a breach of regulation even though standards have been largely complied with. But it must still decide what action, if any, to take. If the standards are persistently flouted and/or they are substantially or seriously disregarded, the NCSC will take enforcement action as outlined above. Even in this event (unless the failing is substantial), there is an opportunity for providers to take action to improve the position before a summons and prosecution ensue, or for an LA to take remedial action.

Consultation

These standards and regulations were produced following widespread consultation nationally, with local authorities, individual fostering services and service users.

Many commentators during consultation considered that the Regulations should use the term 'foster carer' rather than 'foster parent', as the former is normally used. The reason why the Regulations have to continue to use the term 'foster parent' is because that is what is used in the primary legislation, the Children Act 1989.

National Minimum Standards for Fostering Services

Introduction

The national minimum standards for fostering services are issued by the Secretary of State under sections 23 and 49 of the CSA. The Secretary of State will keep the standards under review and may publish amended standards as appropriate.

The fostering services providers to which these standards apply are:

- local authority fostering services
- independent fostering agencies which carry out fostering functions on behalf of local authorities
- voluntary organisations providing fostering services in their own right, under s59 of the Children Act 1989.

They are 'minimum' standards, rather than 'best possible' practice. Many fostering services providers will more than meet the national minimum standards and will aspire to exceed them in many ways. Minimum standards do not mean standardisation of provision. The standards are designed to be applicable to the wide variety of different types of fostering services providers, and to enable rather than prevent individual providers to develop their own particular ethos and approach to care for children with different needs.

Although the standards are issued for use by the NCSC in regulating fostering services providers, they will also have other important practical uses. They may be used by providers and staff in self-assessment of their services, they provide a basis for the induction and training of staff, they can be used by parents, children and young people as a guide to what they should expect a fostering service to provide and to do, and they can provide guidance on what is required when setting up a fostering service. Those involved with fostering services in any way are encouraged to make full use of these standards in these ways.

Structure and approach

The national minimum standards for fostering services focus on achievable outcomes for children and young people – that is, the impact on the individual of the services provided.

The standards are grouped under a series of key topics:

- statement of purpose
- fitness to carry on or manage a fostering service
- management of a fostering service

- securing and promoting welfare
- recruiting, checking, managing, supporting and training staff and foster carers
- records
- fitness of premises
- financial requirements.

Each standard or group of standards is preceded by a statement of the outcome to be achieved by the fostering service provider. The standards themselves are numbered and the full set of numbered paragraphs must be met in order to achieve compliance with the standards. The standards are intended to be qualitative, in that they provide a tool for judging the quality of life experienced by services users, but they are also designed to be measurable.

Wherever possible, the Fostering Services Regulations 2002 (S1 2002 No. 57) that a set of standards is linked to have been listed, under the standards. However, other regulations and/or primary legislation, in particular the Children Act 1989, may also be relevant. The note should be taken as a general guide and is not an exhaustive legal reference.

In inspecting against these standards, the NCSC will follow a consistent inspection methodology and reporting format across the country.

It is intended that the standards will be used, both by fostering services providers and by the NCSC, to focus on securing positive welfare, health and education outcomes for children and young people, and reducing risks to their welfare and safety. All providers and staff of fostering services should aim to provide the best care possible for the children in their care, and observing the standards is an essential part, but only a part, of the overall responsibility to safeguard and promote the welfare of each individual child.

Relationship with UK National Standards for Foster Care

The UK National Standards for Foster Care, produced in 1999, along with the Code of Practice on the recruitment, assessment, approval, training, management and support of foster carers, continue to be applicable to fostering services.

Those Standards are more far-reaching and child-centred – in the sense that they cover all aspects of the life of the foster child, not only the services provided by the fostering service. Although in contrast to the national minimum standards issued under the CSA they have no formal legal status, they represent best practice and as such should be fully complied with by fostering service providers.

1

Statement of Purpose

OUTCOME

There is a clear statement of the aims and objectives of the fostering service and the fostering service ensures that they meet those aims and objectives.

Statement of Purpose

STANDARD 1

1.1 **There is a clear statement of the aims and objectives of the fostering service and of what facilities and services they provide.**

1.2 A statement of purpose clearly sets out what services are provided for children who are placed by the fostering service. If education or health services, including therapeutic services are provided, these are covered in the statement of purpose.

1.3 The registered provider [in the case of a local authority, the elected members] formally approves the statement of purpose of the fostering service, and reviews, updates and modifies it where necessary at least annually.

1.4 The statement includes details in respect of the fostering services of:

- its status and constitution (for agencies)
- its management structure
- the services it provides
- its aims and objectives, principles and standards of care
- numbers, relevant qualifications and experience of staff
- numbers of foster carers
- numbers of children placed
- numbers of complaints and their outcomes
- the procedures and processes for recruiting, approving, training, supporting and reviewing carers.

1.5 The children's guide to the fostering service is suitable for all children fostered through the service, includes a summary of what the service sets out to do for children, and is provided to children as soon as they are fostered, and to all foster carers. (If necessary, the guide is produced in different formats to meet the needs of different groups of children.) The children's guide contains information on how a child can secure access to an independent advocate and about how to complain.

1.6 The fostering service's policies, procedures and any written guidance to staff and carers accurately reflect the statement of purpose.

[Regulation: Statement of purpose and children's guide, Review of statement of purpose and children's guide]

2

Fitness to provide or manage a fostering service

OUTCOME

The fostering service is provided and managed by those with the appropriate skills and experience to do so efficiently and effectively and by those who are suitable to work with children.

Skills to carry on or manage

STANDARD 2

2.1 **The people involved in carrying on and managing the fostering service possess the necessary business and management skills and financial expertise to manage the work efficiently and effectively and have the necessary knowledge and experience of child care and fostering to do so in a professional manner.**

2.2 The manager has:

- a professional qualification relevant to working with children, which must be either NVQ level 4 or the DipSW or another qualification that matches the competencies required by the NVQ Level 4;

- by 2005, a qualification at level 4 NVQ in management or another qualification which matches the competencies required by the NVQ Level 4; and

- at least two years' experience of working with children within the past five years, and in addition at least one year's experience of working at a senior level.

2.3 For the transitional period in relation to management qualifications, appointees to the post of manager who have no such qualifications begin appropriate management training within six months of appointment.

2.4 The manager exercises effective leadership of the staff and operation, such that the fostering service is organised, managed and staffed in a manner that delivers the best possible child care.

Suitability to carry on or manage

STANDARD 3

3.1 **Any persons carrying on or managing the fostering service are suitable people to run a business concerned with safeguarding and promoting the welfare of children.**

3.2 For the references set out in Schedule 1 of the Fostering Services Regulations 2002, telephone enquiries are made to follow up written references.

3.3 Police checks are renewed every three years.

3.4 Records are kept of checks and references that have been obtained and their outcomes.

[Regulations: *Fostering agency: fitness of provider, Fostering agency – fitness of manager, Registered person – general requirements, Local authority fostering service – manager*]

3

Management of the fostering service

OUTCOME

The fostering service is managed ethically and efficiently, delivering a good quality foster care service and avoiding confusion and conflicts of role.

Monitoring and controlling

STANDARD 4

4.1 **There are clear procedures for monitoring and controlling the activities of the fostering service and ensuring quality performance.**

4.2 There are clear roles for managers and staff and well established lines of communication and of accountability between managers, staff and carers.

4.3 The service has proper financial procedures and there is a reviewing procedure to keep them up to date.

4.4 Information is provided to purchasers of services and others. This includes:

- charges for each of its services
- statements of the amounts paid to foster carers, and
- itemised amounts paid for wider services which may include health and education.

4.5 The fostering service informs carers, managers and staff of their responsibility to declare any possible conflicts of interest.

Managing effectively and efficiently

STANDARD 5

5.1 **The fostering service is managed effectively and efficiently.**

5.2 The manager has a clear job description setting out duties and responsibilities and does not hold a similar position in another organisation.

5.3 The level of delegation and responsibility of the manager, and the lines of accountability, are clearly defined.

5.4 Clear arrangements are in place to identify the person in charge when the manager is absent.

[Regulations: *Fostering agency – fitness of provider, Fostering agency – appointment of manager, Fostering agency – fitness of manager, Registered person – general requirements, Local authority fostering service – manager, Fitness of workers, Review of quality of care*]

4

Securing and promoting welfare

OUTCOME

The fostering service promotes and safeguards the child/young person's physical, mental and emotional welfare.

Providing suitable foster carers

STANDARD 6

6.1 The fostering service makes available foster carers who provide a safe, healthy and nurturing environment.

6.2 The foster home can comfortably accommodate all who live there. It is inspected annually to make sure that it meets the needs of foster children.

6.3 The home is warm, adequately furnished and decorated and is maintained to a good standard of cleanliness and hygiene.

6.4 Each child placed has her/his own bed and accommodation arrangements reflect the child's assessed need for privacy and space or for any specific need resulting from a disability.

6.5 If the child has been abused or has abused another child, then the child's needs and the needs of all other children in the home are assessed before any decision is made to allow sharing of bedrooms. The outcome of that assessment is recorded in writing.

6.6 The home and immediate environment are free of avoidable hazards that might expose a child to risk of injury or harm and contain safety barriers and equipment appropriate to the child's age, development and level of ability.

6.7 The foster carer's preparation and training cover health and safety issues and the carer is provided with written guidelines on their health and safety responsibilities.

6.8 Where the foster carer is expected to provide transport for the child, the fostering service ensures this is safe and appropriate to the child's needs.

6.9 Foster carers understand that they may be interviewed or visited as part of the Commission's inspection process.

Valuing diversity

STANDARD 7

7.1 The fostering service ensures that children and young people, and their families, are provided with foster care services which value diversity and promote equality.

7.2 Each child and her/his family have access to foster care services which recognise and address her/his needs in terms of gender, religion, ethnic origin, language, culture, disability and sexuality. If a foster placement has to be made in an emergency and no suitable placement is available in terms of the above, then steps are taken to achieve the above within 6 weeks.

7.3 The fostering service ensures that foster carers and social workers work cooperatively to enhance the child's confidence and feeling of self-worth. Foster carers' and social workers' training covers this issue.

7.4 The fostering service ensures that their foster carers provide care which respects and preserves each child's ethnic, religious, cultural and linguistic background. Foster carers' preparation and training cover this.

7.5 The fostering service ensures that their foster carers support and encourage each child to develop skills to help her/him to deal with all forms of discrimination. Foster carers' preparation and training cover this.

7.6 Each child with a disability receives specific services and support to help her/him to maximise her/his potential and to lead as full a life as possible, including appropriate equipment and, where necessary and appropriate, adaptation of the carer's home and/or vehicle.

7.7 The fostering service ensures that their foster carers give each child encouragement and equal access to opportunities to develop and pursue her/his talents, interests and hobbies. This is set out in the information provided to foster carers. Disabled children are provided with services and supports which enable them to access as wide a range of activities as is possible for them.

Matching

STANDARD 8

8.1 Local authority fostering services, and voluntary agencies placing children in their own right, ensure that each child or young person placed in foster care is carefully matched with a carer capable of meeting her/his assessed needs. For agencies providing foster carers to local authorities, those agencies ensure that they offer carers only if they represent appropriate matches for a child for whom a local authority is seeking a carer.

8.2 In matching children with carers, responsible authorities take into account the child's care plan and recent written assessments of the child and their family and the carers.

8.3 Matches are achieved by means of information sharing and consideration involving all relevant professionals, the child and her/his family and potential carers, their families and other children in placement.

8.4 Written foster placement agreements contain specific reference to elements of matching which were taken into consideration in agreeing the placement and identify areas where foster carers need additional support to compensate for any gaps in the match between the child and carer.

8.5 Placement decisions consider the child's assessed racial, ethnic, religious, cultural and linguistic needs and match these as closely as possible with the ethnic origin, race, religion, culture and language of the foster family.

8.6 Where transracial or transcommunity placements are made, the responsible authority provides the foster family with additional training, support and information to enable the child to be provided with the best possible care and to develop a positive understanding of her/his heritage.

8.7 Where practicable, each child has the opportunity for a period of introduction to a proposed foster carer so she/he can express an informed view about the placement and become familiar with the carer, the carer's family, any other children in placement, and the home, neighbourhood and any family pets, before moving in. Information for carers explains that this approach is used when possible.

Protecting from abuse and neglect

STANDARD 9

9.1 The fostering service protects each child or young person from all forms of abuse, neglect, exploitation and deprivation.

9.2 Training for foster carers includes training in caring for a child who has been abused, safe caring skills, managing behaviour and recognising signs of abuse and on ways of boosting and maintaining the child's self-esteem.

9.3 Safe caring guidelines are provided, based on a written policy, for each foster home, in consultation with the carer and everyone else in the household. The guidelines are cleared with the child's social worker and are explained clearly and appropriately to the child.

9.4 The fostering service makes clear to the foster carers that corporal punishment is not acceptable and that this includes smacking, slapping, shaking and all other humiliating forms of treatment or punishment. This is set out clearly in written information for foster carers.

9.5 Management systems are in place to collate and evaluate information on the circumstances, number and outcome of all allegations of neglect or abuse of a child in foster care. The information is scrutinised regularly.

9.6 The fostering service ensures that foster carers are aware of the particular vulnerability of looked after children and their susceptibility to bullying and procedures are in place to recognise, record and address any instance of bullying and to help foster carers cope with it.

9.7 Each foster carer is provided with full information about the foster child and her/his family to enable the carer to protect the foster child, their own children, other children for whom they have responsibility and themselves.

9.8 The fostering service makes sure that the foster carer has a clear written procedure for use if the foster child is missing from home.

Promoting contact

STANDARD 10

10.1 The fostering service makes sure that each child or young person in foster care is encouraged to maintain and develop family contacts and friendships as set out in her/his care plan and/or foster placement agreement.

10.2 There are clear procedures setting out how appropriate contact arrangements for each child in foster care are to be established, maintained, monitored and reviewed.

10.3 The fostering service considers the need for and benefits of appropriate contact for the child when finding/suggesting a suitable foster carer. Attention is paid to supporting contact where the child is placed outside of the area.

10.4 The views of the child or young person are sought and given weight in determining contact arrangements.

10.5 In assessment and training of carers, the fostering service stresses the importance of foster carers helping a child to maintain appropriate contacts and covers the skills required to encourage and facilitate such contacts.

10.6 Except where an overriding requirement exists, eg a court order, the fostering service ensures that contact does not take place until the child's social worker has carried out a risk assessment and arrangements made for any supervision that is needed.

10.7 The fostering service provides help and support to the carer in dealing with any difficult contact issues that may arise. The fostering service provider ensures that the role of the foster carer in supporting contact arrangements, including any arrangements for the supervision of contact are clearly articulated in the Foster Placement Agreement.

10.8 Financial support is provided to the carer for transport or other costs involved in ensuring contacts take place at the desired frequency and in the most suitable place.

10.9 The fostering service ensures that the carer records outcomes of contact arrangements and their perceived impact on the child; this information is fed back to the child's social worker.

Consultation

STANDARD 11

11.1   **The fostering service ensures that children's opinions, and those of their families and others significant to the child, are sought over all issues which are likely to affect their daily life and their future.**

11.2   The fostering service ensures that all foster carers understand the importance of listening to the views of the children in their care, and are trained and supported in listening and responding to children's views.

11.3   The fostering service ensures that the opinions and views of children on all matters affecting them, including day-to-day matters, are ascertained on a regular and frequent basis and not taken for granted.

11.4   Suitable means are provided, frequently, for any child with communication difficulties to make their wishes and feelings known regarding their care and treatment.

11.5   The fostering service ensures that children in foster care know how to raise any concerns or complaints, and ensures that they receive prompt feedback on any concerns or complaints raised.

Promoting development and health

STANDARD 12

12.1   **The fostering service ensures that it provides foster care services which help each child or young person in foster care to receive health care which meets her/his needs for physical, emotional and social development, together with information and training appropriate to her/his age and understanding to enable informed participation in decisions about her/his health needs.**

12.2   The fostering service is informed about health services, including specialist services, available in the area it covers and takes this into account when finding/suggesting a foster carer for a child. The fostering service ensures that no placement is made which prevents a child from continuing to receive the specialist health care services they need.

12.3   Before a placement begins, the carer is provided with as full a description as possible of the health needs of a child and clear procedures governing consent for the child to receive medical treatment. Where there is an agency placement, the responsible authority provides this information to the agency and the agency passes it on to the carer. If full details of the health needs are not available before placement, a high priority is given to ensuring that the information is obtained and passed to the foster carer once the placement is made.

12.4 The carer is provided with a written health record for each child placed in their care; this is updated during the placement and moves with the child. Depending upon age and understanding, the child has access to and understands the health record kept by the fostering service.

12.5 Each carer is given basic training on health and hygiene issues and first aid, with particular emphasis on health promotion and communicable diseases.

12.6 The fostering service makes clear to the carer their role in terms of helping to promote the health of any child in their care. This includes:

- registering a child with a doctor or dentist when necessary
- taking the child to any health appointments, including dental and optician appointments, when required
- helping her/him to access the services that she/he needs
- giving attention to health issues in everyday care of the child, including diet, personal hygiene, health promotion issues etc
- acting as an advocate on the child's behalf.

12.7 The fostering service has good links with health agencies and helps the carer to secure services for the child when necessary.

12.8 The fostering service requires foster carers to supply information about the child's health needs for the planning and review process.

Promoting educational achievement

STANDARD 13

13.1 The fostering service gives a high priority to meeting the educational needs of each child or young person in foster care and ensures that she/he is encouraged to attain her/his full potential

13.2 The fostering service gives high priority to helping their foster carers to meet a child's education needs.

13.3 The fostering service requires foster carers to contribute to the assessment of the child's educational needs and progress for the planning and review process. The fostering service helps the foster carer to contribute to the delivery of any personal education plan.

13.4 The foster carer's role in school contact, e.g., parents evenings, open days, discussions with teachers, in conjunction with the birth parent where appropriate and in line with the care plan, is clearly laid out in the placement agreement.

13.5 The fostering service ensures that their foster carers provide an environment in which education and learning are valued; and that the foster carer establishes an expectation of regular attendance at school, and supports the child's full participation through provision of necessary uniform and equipment, support for completion of homework, and financial and other support for attending school trips and after school activities.

13.6 The fostering service has information systems to demonstrate the educational attainment of the children and young people in their foster care services and to demonstrate the numbers excluded from school.

13.7 The fostering service makes clear its expectations (in relation to school-day responsibilities) of foster carers and the arrangements which will be put in place if any child in their care is not in school. Those arrangements include structured occupation during school hours.

13.8 The foster placement agreement identifies where financial responsibility lies for all school costs, including school uniform, school trips and school equipment.

Preparing for adulthood

STANDARD 14

14.1 **The fostering service ensures that their foster care services help to develop skills, competence and knowledge necessary for adult living.**

14.2 There are clear written requirements of what is expected of foster carers in terms of preparing children and young people for independent or semi-independent living.

14.3 Foster carers receive training and support to enable them to provide effective support and guidance to a young person preparing to move into independent or semi-independent living.

14.4 The fostering service ensures that foster carers understand that they need to provide all children in their care with age and developmentally appropriate opportunities for learning independence skills.

14.5 The fostering service ensures that each young person preparing to move to independent or semi-independent living is consulted about her/his future and encouraged to be actively involved in decision making processes and implementation of the Pathway Plan.

[Regulations: *Independent fostering agencies – duty to secure welfare, Arrangements for the protection of children, Behaviour management and absence from foster parent's home, Duty to promote contact, Health of children placed with foster parents, Education, employment and leisure activities, Independent fostering agencies – complaints and representations*]

5

Recruiting, checking, managing, supporting and training staff and foster carers

OUTCOME

The people who work in or for the fostering service are suitable to work with children and young people and they are managed, trained and supported in such a way as to ensure the best possible outcomes for children in foster care. The number of staff and carers and their range of qualifications and experience are sufficient to achieve the purposes and functions of the organisation.

Suitability to work with children

STANDARD 15

15.1 **Any people working in or for the fostering service are suitable people to work with children and young people and to safeguard and promote their welfare.**

15.2 There are clear written recruitment and selection procedures for appointing staff which follow good practice in safeguarding children and young people. All personnel responsible for recruitment and selection of staff are trained in, understand and operate these.

15.3 All people working in or for the fostering service are interviewed as part of the selection process and have references checked to assess suitability before taking on responsibilities. Telephone enquiries are made as well as obtaining written references.

15.4 Records are kept of checks and references that have been obtained and their outcomes. Police checks are renewed every three years.

15.5 All social work staff have an appropriate qualification, or are in the course of obtaining a suitable professional qualification, to work with children and young people, their families and foster carers, and have a good understanding of foster care. They have appropriate knowledge and skills. These include:

- understanding of the Children Act, the Children Act regulations and guidance, relevant current policies and procedures, Working Together and associated child protection guidance, the Framework for the Assessment of Children in Need and their Families, the regulatory requirements under the Care Standards Act 2000 and adoption law

- knowledge of the growth and development of children and an ability to communicate with children and young people
- understanding the importance of a complaints procedure
- an ability to promote equality, diversity and the rights of individuals and groups
- knowledge of the roles of other agencies, in particular health and education.

15.6 Any social work staff involved in assessment and approval of foster carers are qualified social workers, have experience of foster care and family placement work and are trained in assessment. Students and others who do not meet this requirement carry out assessments and approvals under the supervision of someone who does, who takes responsibility for the assessments and approvals.

15.7 All educationalists, psychologists, therapists and other professional staff are professionally qualified and appropriately trained to work with children and young people, their families and foster carers, and have a good understanding of foster care.

15.8 Where unqualified staff carry out social work functions they do so under the direct supervision of qualified social workers, who are accountable for their work.

Organisation and management of staff

STANDARD 16

16.1 Staff are organised and managed in a way which delivers an efficient and effective foster care service.

16.2 There is a clear management structure with clear lines of accountability.

16.3 Staff are managed and monitored by people who have appropriate skills and qualifications.

16.4 The level of management delegation and responsibility are clearly defined and are appropriate for the skills, qualifications and experience of the relevant members of staff.

16.5 The fostering service has systems in place to determine, prioritise and monitor workloads and assign tasks to appropriate staff.

16.6 There are structures and systems in place to ensure assessments, approvals and reviews of carers are managed and implemented effectively. Local authorities using agencies check the Commission inspection reports before doing so, to ensure that there are no concerns about the agencies' assessment, approval and review processes.

16.7 Where a local authority fostering service uses an agency to provide a foster carer, they have a system to ensure that the quality of care to be provided is clearly specified in the contract and appropriate monitoring arrangements are in place to ensure compliance.

16.8 Professional supervision and consultation are provided for social work staff by appropriately qualified and experienced staff.

16.9 Staff and carers undertake on-going training and appropriate professional and skills development. Carers maintain a training portfolio.

16.10 There is adequate administrative back up, office equipment, and infrastructure to enable staff who recruit, assess, supervise, support and train foster carers to carry out their duties in an efficient and effective manner.

16.11 There is an appropriate level of clerical and administrative support.

16.12 Administrative procedures are appropriate for dealing promptly with enquiries from prospective carers and any new request for services.

16.13 There is access to the range of advice needed to provide a full service for children and young people and to support carers. This includes appropriate childcare, medical, educational and other professional and legal advice.

16.14 All employees, sessional workers and consultants are provided with appropriate written contracts, job descriptions and conditions of service.

16.15 All fostering service social workers understand the role of the children's social workers, and there is a clear understanding about how the fostering service social workers and the children's social workers work effectively together.

16.16 Staff have a copy of:

- the policies and working practices in respect of grievances and disciplinary matters
- details of the services offered
- the equal opportunities policy
- health and safety procedures.

Sufficient staff/carers with the right skills/experience

STANDARD 17

17.1 The fostering service has an adequate number of sufficiently experienced and qualified staff and recruits a range of carers to meet the needs of children and young people for whom it aims to provide a service.

17.2 The full time equivalent staffing complement, in terms of numbers, grades, experience and qualifications, is adequate to meet, at all times, the needs of the fostering service and is line with the statement of purpose.

17.3 Where a shortfall in staffing levels occurs, there are contingency plans to resolve the situation.

17.4 Staff policies encourage retention of salaried staff – including training, regular supervision, study leave, clear workloads and terms and conditions – and of carers by providing support, training and services.

17.5 The fostering service has a recruitment policy and strategy aimed at recruiting a range of carers to meet the needs of children and young people for whom it aims to provide a service.

17.6 There is a clearly set out assessment process for carers which defines:

- the task to be undertaken
- the qualities, competences or aptitudes being sought or to be achieved
- the standards to be applied in the assessment
- the stages and content of the selection process and the timescales involved
- the information to be given to applicants.

17.7 In assessing qualities, competences and aptitudes for fostering, fostering services consider them in relation to the following:

- child rearing
- caring for children born to somebody else
- contact between fostered children and their families
- helping children make sense of their past
- sexual boundaries and attitudes
- awareness of issues around child abuse
- approaches to discipline
- awareness of how to promote secure attachments between children and appropriate adults
- awareness of own motivation for fostering/own needs to be met through the fostering process
- religion
- racial/cultural/linguistic issues
- standard of living and lifestyle
- health
- own experience of parenting and being parented
- own experiences in relation to disability and/or attitudes to disability.

Fair and competent employer

STANDARD 18

18.1 The fostering service is a fair and competent employer, with sound employment practices and good support for its staff and carers.

18.2 There are sound employment practices, in relation to both staff and carers.

18.3 Out of hours management and support services are available for foster carers.

18.4 There are management systems for carer supervision, appraisal and support.

18.5   There is a comprehensive health and safety policy for carers, children and staff which covers all legal requirements.

18.6   For agencies, there is a public liability and professional indemnity insurance for all staff and carers. The insurance policy covers costs arising as a result of child abuse claims against any staff or carers.

18.7   There is a whistleblowing policy which is made known to all staff and carers.

Training

STANDARD 19

19.1   There is a good quality training programme to enhance individual skills and to keep staff up-to-date with professional and legal developments.

19.2   There is a clear plan for the training and development of all staff involved in fostering work through induction, post-qualifying and in-service training. All new staff are given induction training commencing within 7 days of starting their employment and being completed within 10 weeks.

19.3   There is an appraisal or joint review scheme which identifies the training and development needs of all staff involved in fostering work and carers. Individual programmes of training are available, outcomes are monitored and linked to assessment of staff and carer needs, and relate to the tasks assigned to them.

19.4   All employees are kept informed of changes in any legislation or guidance that are relevant to their jobs.

19.5   The effectiveness of training programmes for the staff providing the fostering service is routinely evaluated and training programmes are reviewed and updated at least annually.

19.6   Training programmes reflect the policies of the fostering service.

19.7   Joint training between fostering service staff and foster carers is held on a regular basis.

Accountability and support

STANDARD 20

20.1   All staff are properly accountable and supported.

20.2   All staff have clear written details of the duties and responsibilities expected of them, together with the policies and procedures of the organisation.

20.3   All staff who come into contact with foster carers and prospective foster carers and children/young people receive management supervision and a record is kept by the line manager of the content of the supervision and of progress made. Supervision sessions are regular and planned in advance.

20.4   Staff receive regular, planned appraisals from their line manager.

20.5 Each member of staff has the opportunity to attend regular staff and team meetings.

Management and support of carers

STANDARD 21

21.1 The fostering service has a clear strategy for working with and supporting carers.

21.2 There is a clear strategy for working with carers that is documented and understood. This includes:

- arrangements for training and development
- encouragement for self help groups
- supervision
- support services
- *information and advice*
- assistance in dealing with other relevant services, such as health and education
- out-of-hours support
- respite care
- arrangements for reviews.

21.5 The role of the supervising social worker is clear both to the worker and the carer. Annual review reports are prepared and are available to the Fostering Panel.

21.6 There is a good system of communication between the fostering service social workers and the child's social worker.

Supervision of carers

STANDARD 22

22. 1 The fostering service is a managed one which provides supervision for foster carers and helps them to develop their skills.

22.2 Foster care agreements ensure foster carers have a full understanding of what is expected of foster carers, the agency and/or the local authority.

22.3 Each approved foster carer is supervised by a named, appropriately qualified social worker and has access to adequate social work and other professional support, information and advice to enable her or him to provide consistent, high quality care for a child or young person placed in her or his home. The supervising social worker ensures each carer she or he supervises is informed in writing of, and accepts, understands and operates within, all standards, policies and guidance agreed by the fostering service.

22.4   In producing the Foster Care Agreement for a foster carer, in line with Schedule 5 of the Fostering Services Regulations 2001, the fostering provider ensures that the Agreement contains the information they need to know, in a comprehensible style, to carry out their functions as a foster carer effectively.

22.5   On approval, carers are given a handbook which covers policies, procedures, guidance, legal information and insurance details. This is updated regularly.

22.6   Supervising social workers meet regularly with foster carers. Meetings have a clear purpose and provide the opportunity to supervise the foster carers' work. Foster carers' files include records of supervisory meetings. There are occasional unannounced visits, at least one each year.

22.7   There is a system of practical support for carers, including:

- out of hours management support
- prompt payment
- insurance cover
- support for foster care associations
- respite care where appropriate
- access to social work support.

22.8   Information about the procedures for dealing with complaints and representations is widely available. Complaints and representations are recorded and monitored and the outcome evaluated to inform future provision of services.

22.9   Information about the procedures to deal with investigations into allegations is made known to foster care staff, carers and children and young people and includes the provision of independent support to the foster carer(s) during an investigation.

22.10   Records about allegations of abuse are kept and monitored and there is a clear policy framework which outlines the circumstances in which a carer should be removed from the foster carer register.

Training of carers

STANDARD 23

23.1   The fostering service ensures that foster carers are trained in the skills required to provide high quality care and meet the needs of each child/young person placed in their care.

23.2   Pre-approval and induction training for each carer includes opportunities to benefit from the experience and knowledge of existing carers. All new foster carers receive induction training.

23.3 All training fits within a framework of equal opportunities, anti-discriminatory practice and is organised to encourage and facilitate attendance by foster carers, for example by including convenient times and venues and by providing childcare and reasonable expenses.

23.4 Where two adults in one household are approved as joint carers, both successfully complete all training. Each foster carer is trained in identified key areas prior to any child being placed in his or her home. Attention is given to the training needs of particular groups, eg male carers.

23.5 There is an on-going programme of training and self-development for foster carers to develop their skills and tackle any weaknesses.

23.6 Appropriate training on safe caring is provided for all members of the foster household.

23.7 Specific consideration is given to any help or support needed by the sons and daughters of foster carers.

23.8 Each carer's Annual Review includes an appraisal of training and development needs, which is documented in the review report.

23.9 The effectiveness of training received is evaluated and reviewed annually.

[Regulations: *Support, training and information for foster parents, Staffing of fostering service, Fitness of workers, Employment of staff, Assessment of prospective foster parents, Approval of foster parents*]

6

Records

In meeting these standards in relation to record-keeping, it may well be that local authority fostering services maintain some of the records within the part of the social services department that is responsible for supervising the child's placement, rather than the fostering services. Nothing in these standards requires two separate parts of the social services department to maintain duplicate sets of records, as long as both parts have access to the records.

OUTCOME

All appropriate records are kept and are accessible in relation to the fostering services and the individual foster carers and foster children.

Case records for children

STANDARD 24

24.1 **The fostering service ensures that an up-to-date, comprehensive case record is maintained for each child or young person in foster care which details the nature and quality of care provided and contributes to an understanding of her/his life events. Relevant information from the case records is made available to the child and to anyone involved in her/his care.**

24.2 There is a written policy on case recording which establishes the purpose, format and contents of files, and clarifies what information is kept on the foster carer's files and what information is kept on the child's files.

24.3 Where there is an agency placement the agency works with the responsible authority to ensure effective integration of information held in the agency's case files and those of the responsible authority. The agency provides copies of the records and documents in relation to children placed by a responsible authority immediately, on receipt of a written request. When a child leaves an agency foster care placement, the agency sends all relevant records to the responsible authority.

24.4 The fostering service ensures that the foster carer knows why the child is in foster care and understands the basis for the current placement, its intended duration and purpose, and the details of the child's legal status.

24.5 The foster carer encourages the child to reflect on and understand her/his history, according to the child's age and ability, and to keep appropriate memorabilia. The fostering service makes this role clear to their foster carers.

24.6 The fostering service gives the foster carer access to all relevant information to help the child understand and come to terms with past events. (Where necessary information is not forthcoming from the responsible authority, a copy of the written request for information is kept.)

24.7 The carer is trained and provided with the necessary equipment to record significant life events for the child, and to encourage the child to make such recordings, including photograph albums.

24.8 The fostering service ensures that their carers store information in a secure manner and understand what information they are expected to keep and what information needs to be passed on to the fostering service.

Administrative records

STANDARD 25

25.1 The fostering service's administrative records contain all significant information relevant to the running of the foster care service and as required by regulations.

25.2 Separate records are kept for:

- staff, employed and independent/sessional
- carers
- children
- complaints
- allegations.

25.3 There is a system to monitor the quality and adequacy of records, and remedial action is taken when necessary.

25.4 Confidential records are stored securely at all times and there is a clear policy on access.

25.5 Records are in a form which can be readily passed on if a child moves to another placement, or ceases to be looked after or if references are requested on a member of staff or carer.

25.6 There is a permanent, private, secure record for each child and foster carer referred to or appointed by the organisation. This can, in compliance with legal requirements for safeguards, be seen by the child and by her/his parents or foster carers.

25.7 There is a written policy and procedural guidance for staff for the keeping and retention of case files ensuring that foster carers, fostered children and their parents know the nature of the records maintained and how to access them.

25.8 There is a procedure on storing and managing confidential information that is known to panel members, staff and specialist advisers.

25.9   Written entries in records are legible, clearly expressed, non-stigmatising, and distinguish between fact, opinion and third party information.

25.10   The system for keeping records is congruent with the Looking After Children System/Integrated Children's System.

25.11   Records are kept of checks and references that have been obtained and their outcomes.

25.12   Children and foster carers are encouraged to access their records, make additions and comments and record personal statements, including any dissent.

25.13   There is a system for keeping records about allegations and complaints and for handling these confidentially and securely. Records of complaints and allegations are clearly recorded on the relevant files for staff, carers and children – including details of the investigation, conclusion reached and action taken. Separate records are also kept which bring together data on allegations and on complaints.

[Regulations: *Records with respect to fostering services, Case records relating to foster parents and others*]

7

Fitness of premises for use as fostering service

> **OUTCOME**
>
> The premises used as offices by the fostering provider are suitable for the purpose.

Premises

STANDARD 26

26.1 **Premises used as offices by the fostering service are appropriate for the purpose.**

26.2 There are identifiable office premises to which staff and others with a legitimate interest have access during normal office hours.

26.3 There are efficient and robust administrative systems, including IT and communication systems. Premises have:

- facilities for the secure retention of records in a lockable room
- appropriate measures to safeguard IT systems and
- an appropriate security system.

26.4 Premises provide an equipped base from which staff work.

26.5 The premises and its contents are adequately insured (or there are alternative prompt methods of replacing lost items).

[Regulation: *Fitness of premises*]

8

Financial requirements

OUTCOME

The agency fostering services are financially viable and appropriate and timely payments are made to foster carers.

Financial viability

STANDARD 27

27.1 **The agency ensures it is financially viable at all times and has sufficient financial resources to fulfil its obligations.**

27.2 Procedures exist to deal with situations of financial crisis, such as disclosing information to purchasers and liaising with them to safeguard the welfare of children receiving services through the agency.

27.3 Regulations and guidelines imposed upon businesses are conformed with. This includes Income Tax (PAYE), National Insurance and VAT.

Financial processes

STANDARD 28

28.1 **The financial processes/systems of the agency are properly operated and maintained in accordance with sound and appropriate accounting standards and practice.**

28.2 The agency has clearly documented financial arrangements for control and supervision of its financial affairs and powers.

28.3 The agency has a clearly written set of principles and standards governing its financial management and these are communicated to its managers and accountants.

28.4 The agency has a written set of principles describing the financial procedures and responsibilities to be followed by all staff, consultants, professional experts, directors, trustees and any manager.

28.5 The agency's accounts are maintained and properly audited by a registered accountant.

28.6 The registered provider regularly receives information on the financial state of the agency.

28.7 The agency publishes its charges for each of its services and has a clear policy for the charging of fees and expenses for any additional services it is asked to provide. The statement is available on request to purchasers and others with a legitimate interest.

Payment to carers

STANDARD 29

29.1 Each foster carer receives an allowance and agreed expenses, which cover the full cost of caring for each child or young person placed with him or her. Payments are made promptly and at the agreed time. Allowances and fees are reviewed annually.

29.2 There is a written policy on fostering allowances. This and the current allowance levels are well publicised and provided annually to each carer. The carer receives clear information about the allowances and expenses payable and how to access them, before a child is placed.

[Regulation: *Financial position*]

9 Fostering panels

OUTCOME

Fostering panels are organised efficiently and effectively so as to ensure that good quality decisions are made about the approval of foster carers, in line with the overriding objective to promote and safeguard the welfare of children in foster care.

STANDARD 30

30.1 Fostering panels have clear written policies and procedures, which are implemented in practice, about the handling of their functions.

30.2 The written procedures cover decision-making when all members of the panel are not in agreement.

30.3 There are requirements about suitability of foster panel members, including Criminal Record Bureau checks. No panel members are allowed to begin work until all checks have been satisfactorily completed.

30.4 Fostering panels have access to medical expertise as required.

30.5 Fostering panels provide a quality assurance function in relation to the assessment process – in particular to monitor and review the work of the assessors; to provide feedback; to identify problems; and to ensure that there is consistency of approach in assessment across the service, that it is fair to all applicants and that it has been completed in a thorough and rigorous way.

30.6 Foster panels receive management information about the outcome of foster carers' annual reviews.

30.7 For local authority panels, the panel monitors the range and type of carers available to the authority in comparison with the needs of children.

30.8 The independent members of the panel include, as far as possible, expertise in education and in child health.

30.9 One of the independent members is normally a person who has at any time been placed with foster carers or whose child has at any time been placed with foster carers.

[Regulations: *Establishment of fostering panel, Meetings of fostering panel, Functions of fostering panel*]

10
Short-term breaks

OUTCOME

When foster care is provided as a short-term break for a child, the arrangements recognise that the parents remain the main carers for the child.

STANDARD 31

31.1 **Where a fostering service provides short-term breaks for children in foster care, they have policies and procedures, implemented in practice, to meet the particular needs of children receiving short-term breaks.**

31.2 Where appropriate, requirements for foster care placements for short-term breaks are different from those for children being fostered for longer periods. In particular, birth parents remain central to the promotion of health and education needs.

11 Family and friends as carers

OUTCOME

Local authority fostering services' policies and procedures for assessing, approving, supporting and training foster carers recognise the particular contribution that can be made by and the particular needs of family and friends as carers.

STANDARD 32

32.1 These standards are all relevant to carers who are family and friends of the child, but there is a recognition of the particular relationship and position of family and friends carers.

32.2 Local authority fostering services are sensitive to pre-existing relationships in assessing and approving family and friends as foster carers.

32.3 The support and training needs for family and friends carers are assessed and met in the same way as for any other carers.

32.4 The mechanisms within a local authority fostering service for assessing and approving family and friend carers are designed in a way that encourages their consideration as carers.

Appendices

Glossary

This glossary is intended to be of general assistance to the reader in interpreting the standards. The definitions provided do not affect any meaning that a term may have under any relevant legislation.

Abuse

Something that causes actual or likely significant harm to a child. May be physical, emotional or sexual, or neglect of the child.

Advocate

A person assisting a child in putting forward their views or making their case on their behalf.

Bullying

Generally, bullying would comprise the intentional or perceived causing of pain, distress, anxiety, humiliation or social exclusion to one child by one or more other children, by physical or verbal means, or through damage or loss of property.

Care plan

An agreed plan for looking after a child and meeting that child's current and future needs, made by the placing authority under the Children Act 1989.

Child protection

Taking reasonable measures to reduce the risk of physical, emotional or sexual abuse, neglect or significant harm of a child, enabling children or staff to report concerns about actual or potential abuse or significant harm, and responding appropriately to allegations, occurrences and suspicions of abuse or significant harm of a child.

Criminal Records Bureau

A national organisation conducting police checks to enable an assessment to be made (eg by a school) on the suitability of a person to work with children. Different levels of check are available for different levels of regular contact and supervisory responsibility for children.

Induction

Initial training or guidance given at the start of involvement with a fostering services provider.

Job Description

A written, agreed and up to date statement of the main tasks and responsibilities of a staff member's job within the fostering service, including overall definition of their role and the person to whom they are accountable.

Neglect

Single or repeated failure to take appropriate action which results in harm or distress being suffered by the child or young person.

Placement

The agreement for a child to live in a particular place.

Policy

An operational statement of intent which helps staff make sound decisions and take actions which are legal, consistent with the aims of the fostering service, and in the best interests of children and young people.

Procedure

The steps taken to fulfil a policy.

Registered person

A person who either provides a fostering service (through an agency) and is registered with the National Care Standards Commission to do so (the registered provider) or who manages the service and is registered with the Commission to do so (the registered manager).

Staff

Person working in the fostering service or on behalf of the service, whether paid or voluntary, full-time or part-time, casual, agency or contract.

Statement of purpose

A document required by the Regulations which defines the objectives of the fostering service, and covers those issues set out in the Regulations and national minimum standards.

Welfare

Meeting each individual child's reasonable physical, security, personal, emotional, and spiritual needs, providing support and guidance as needed, and enabling the child's development for the future and fulfilment in the present, taking into account the child's age, characteristics and wishes.

Bibliography

UK Joint Working Party on Foster Care, *Code of practice on the recruitment, assessment, approval, training, management and support of foster carers.* London: National Foster Care Association 1999. ISBN: 189788869274

UK Joint Working Party on Foster Care, *UK National Standards for foster care.* London: National Foster Care Association 1999. ISBN: 1897869266

Fostering Services
Regulations 2002

STATUTORY INSTRUMENTS

2002 No. 57

SOCIAL CARE, ENGLAND
CHILDREN AND YOUNG PERSONS, ENGLAND

The Fostering Services Regulations 2002

Made - - - - -	*14th January 2002*
Laid before Parliament	*15th January 2002*
Coming into force - -	*1st April 2002*

ARRANGEMENT OF REGULATIONS

PART IV

APPROVAL OF FOSTER PARENTS

PART V

PLACEMENTS

PART VI

LOCAL AUTHORITY VISITS

PART VII

FOSTERING AGENCIES—MISCELLANEOUS

PART VIII

MISCELLANEOUS

SCHEDULES

The Secretary of State in exercise of the powers conferred upon him by sections 22(1), (2)(a) to (c), (e) to (j), (6), (7)(a) to (h), (j), 25(1), 34(1), 48(1), 52(1), 118(5) to (7) of the Care Standards Act 2000(**a**) and sections 23(2)(a) and (9), 59(2) and 62(3) of, and paragraph 12 of Schedule 2 to, the Children Act 1989(**b**) and of all other powers enabling him in that behalf and having consulted such persons as he considers appropriate(**c**), hereby makes the following Regulations:—

PART I

GENERAL

Citation, commencement and extent

1.—(1) These Regulations may be cited as the Fostering Services Regulations 2002 and shall come into force on 1st April 2002.

(2) These Regulations extend to England only.

Interpretation

2.—(1) In these Regulations, unless the context otherwise requires—

"the 1989 Act" means the Children Act 1989;

"the 2000 Act" means the Care Standards Act 2000;

"approval" means approval as a foster parent in accordance with regulation 28 and references to a person being approved shall be construed accordingly;

"area authority" means the local authority in whose area a child is placed, in any case where that local authority is not the child's responsible authority;

"assessment" shall be construed in accordance with regulation 27(l);

"child protection enquiries" has the meaning given to it by regulation 12(4);

"children's guide" means the written guide produced in accordance with regulation 3(3);

"foster care agreement" has the meaning given to it by regulation 28(5)(b);

(**a**) 2000 c. 14. These powers are exercisable by the appropriate Minister, who is defined in section 121(1) of the Care Standards Act, in relation to England, Scotland and Northern Ireland, as the Secretary of State, and in relation to Wales, as the National Assembly for Wales. "Prescribed" and "regulations" are defined in section 121(1) of that Act.

(**b**) 1989 c. 41. These powers are exercisable by the Secretary of State in relation to England. Their exercise in relation to Wales has been transferred to the National Assembly for Wales by virtue of article 2 of, and the entry for the Children Act 1989 in Schedule 1 to, the National Assembly for Wales (Transfer of Functions) Order 1999 (S.I. 1999/672).

(**c**) *See* section 22(9) of the Care Standards Act 2000 for the requirement to consult.

"foster placement agreement" has the meaning given to it by regulation 34(3);

"foster parent" means a person with whom a child is placed or may be placed under these Regulations, and except in Parts IV and V of these Regulations, includes any person who is not a foster parent but with whom a child is placed by a local authority under regulation 38(2);

"fostering panel" means a panel established in accordance with regulation 24;

"fostering service" means—

(a) a fostering agency within the meaning of section 4(4) of the 2000 Act; or

(b) a local authority fostering service;

"fostering service provider" means—

(a) in relation to a fostering agency, a registered person; or

(b) in relation to a local authority fostering service, a local authority;

"general practitioner" means a registered medical practitioner who—

(a) provides general medical services under Part II of the National Health Service Act 1977(**a**);

(b) performs personal medical services in connection with a pilot scheme under the National Health Service (Primary Care) Act 1997(**b**); or

(c) provides services which correspond to services provided under Part II of the National Health Service Act 1977 otherwise than in pursuance of that Act;

"independent fostering agency" means a fostering agency falling within section 4(4)(a) of the 2000 Act (discharging functions of local authorities in connection with the placing of children with foster parents);

"local authority fostering service" means the discharge by a local authority of relevant fostering functions within the meaning of section 43(3)(b) of the 2000 Act;

"organisation" means a body corporate or any unincorporated association other than a partnership;

"parent" in relation to a child, includes any person who has parental responsibility for him;

"placement" means any placement of a child made by—

(a) a local authority under section 23(2)(a) of the 1989 Act or a voluntary organisation under section 59(1)(a) of the 1989 Act which is not—

(i) a placement with a person who falls within section 23(4) of that Act; or

(ii) a placement for adoption; and

(b) except in Part V of these Regulations includes a placement arranged by an independent fostering agency acting on behalf of a local authority,

and references to a child who is placed shall be construed accordingly;

"registered manager" in relation to a fostering agency means a person who is registered under Part II of the 2000 Act as the manager of the fostering agency;

"registered person" in relation to a fostering agency means any person who is the registered provider or the registered manager of the fostering agency;

"registered provider" in relation to a fostering agency means a person who is registered under Part II of the 2000 Act as the person carrying on the fostering agency(**c**);

"responsible authority" means, in relation to a child, the local authority or voluntary organisation as the case may be, responsible for the child's placement;

"responsible individual" shall be construed in accordance with regulation 5(2)(c)(i);

"statement of purpose" means the written statement compiled in accordance with regulation 3(1).

(2) In these Regulations, a reference—

(a) to a numbered regulation or Schedule is to the regulation in, or Schedule to, these Regulations bearing that number;

(**a**) 1977 c. 49.

(**b**) 1997 c. 46.

(**c**) By section 121(4) of the 2000 Act the person who carries on a fostering agency falling within section 4(4)(b) of that Act (a voluntary organisation which places children with foster parents under section 59(1) of the 1989 Act) is the voluntary organisation itself.

(b) in a regulation or Schedule to a numbered paragraph, is to the paragraph in that regulation or Schedule bearing that number;

(c) in a paragraph to a lettered or numbered sub-paragraph is to the sub-paragraph in that paragraph bearing that letter or number.

(3) In these Regulations, references to employing a person include employing a person whether or not for payment, and whether under a contract of service or a contract for services, and allowing a person to work as a volunteer, but do not include allowing a person to act as a foster parent, and references to an employee or to a person being employed shall be construed accordingly.

Statement of purpose and children's guide

3.—(1) The fostering service provider shall compile, in relation to the fostering service, a written statement (in these Regulations referred to as "the statement of purpose") which shall consist of—

(a) a statement of the aims and objectives of the fostering service; and

(b) a statement as to the services and facilities to be provided by the fostering service.

(2) The fostering service provider shall provide a copy of the statement of purpose to the Commission(a) and shall make it available, upon request, for inspection by—

(a) any person working for the purposes of the fostering service;

(b) any foster parent or prospective foster parent of the fostering service;

(c) any child placed with a foster parent by the fostering service; and

(d) the parent of any such child.

(3) The fostering service provider shall produce a written guide to the fostering service (in these Regulations referred to as "the children's guide") which shall include—

(a) a summary of the statement of purpose;

(b) a summary of the procedure established—

(i) in the case of an independent fostering agency, under regulation 18(1);

(ii) in the case of a local authority fostering service, under section 26(3) of the 1989 Act; and

(iii) in the case of a fostering agency falling within section 4(4)(b) of the 2000 Act, under section 59(4)(b) of the 1989 Act(b); and

(c) the address and telephone number of the Commission.

(4) The fostering service provider shall provide a copy of the children's guide to the Commission, to each foster parent approved by the fostering service provider and (subject to his age and understanding), to each child placed by it.

(5) Subject to paragraph (6) of this regulation the fostering service provider shall ensure that the fostering service is at all times conducted in a manner which is consistent with its statement of purpose.

(6) Nothing in paragraph (5) shall require or authorise the fostering service provider to contravene or not comply with—

(a) any other provision of these Regulations; or

(b) in the case of a fostering agency, any conditions for the time being in force in relation to the registration of the registered person under Part II of the 2000 Act.

Review of statement of purpose and children's guide

4. The fostering service provider shall—

(a) keep under review and where appropriate revise the statement of purpose and children's guide;

(b) notify the Commission of any such revision within 28 days; and

(a) By virtue of section 6(1) of the 2000 Act, the Commission means the National Care Standards Commission established under that Act.
(b) The current Regulations are the Representations Procedure (Children) Regulations 1991 (S.I. 1991/894, as amended by S.I. 1991/2033, S.I. 1993/3069, and S.I. 2001/2874).

(c) if the children's guide is revised, supply a copy to each foster parent approved by the fostering service provider and (subject to his age and understanding), to each child placed by it.

PART II

REGISTERED PERSONS AND MANAGEMENT OF LOCAL AUTHORITY FOSTERING SERVICE

Fostering agency—fitness of provider

5.—(1) A person shall not carry on a fostering agency unless he is fit to do so.

(2) A person is not fit to carry on a fostering agency unless the person—

(a) in the case of an independent fostering agency, is an individual who carries on the fostering agency—

(i) otherwise than in partnership with others and he satisfies the requirements set out in paragraph (3);

(ii) in partnership with others, and he and each of his partners satisfies the requirements set out in paragraph (3);

(b) is a partnership, and each of the partners satisfies the requirements set out in paragraph (3);

(c) is an organisation and—

(i) the organisation has given notice to the Commission of the name, address and position in the organisation of an individual (in these Regulations referred to as "the responsible individual") who is a director, manager, secretary or other officer of the organisation and is responsible for supervising the management of the fostering agency; and

(ii) that individual satisfies the requirements set out in paragraph (3).

(3) The requirements are that—

(a) he is of integrity and good character;

(b) he is physically and mentally fit to carry on the fostering agency; and

(c) full and satisfactory information is available in relation to him—

(i) except where paragraph (4) applies, in respect of each of the matters specified in paragraphs 1 to 6 of Schedule 1;

(ii) where paragraph (4) applies, in respect of each of the matters specified in paragraphs 1 and 3 to 7 of Schedule 1.

(4) This paragraph applies where any certificate or information on any matters referred to in paragraph 2 of Schedule 1 is not available to an individual because any provision of the Police Act 1997(**a**) has not been brought into force.

(5) A person shall not carry on a fostering agency if—

(a) he has been adjudged bankrupt or sequestration of his estate has been awarded and (in either case) he has not been discharged and the bankruptcy order has not been annulled or rescinded; or

(b) he has made a composition or arrangement with his creditors and has not been discharged in respect of it.

Fostering agency—appointment of manager

6.—(1) The registered provider shall appoint an individual to manage the fostering agency.

(2) Where the registered provider is—

(a) an organisation, it shall not appoint the person who is the responsible individual as the manager;

(b) a partnership, it shall not appoint any of the partners as the manager.

(**a**) 1997 c. 50. *See* the footnotes to paragraph 2 of Schedule 1.

(3) The registered provider shall forthwith notify the Commission of—

  (a) the name of any person appointed in accordance with this regulation; and

  (b) the date on which the appointment is to take effect.

Fostering agency—fitness of manager

7.—(1) A person shall not manage a fostering agency unless he is fit to do so.

(2) A person is not fit to manage a fostering agency unless—

  (a) he is of integrity and good character;

  (b) having regard to the size of the fostering agency, its statement of purpose, and the numbers and needs of the children placed by it—

    (i) he has the qualifications, skills and experience necessary for managing the fostering agency; and

    (ii) he is physically and mentally fit to manage a fostering agency;

  (c) full and satisfactory information is available in relation to him—

    (i) except where paragraph (3) applies in respect of each of the matters specified in paragraphs 1 to 6 of Schedule 1;

    (ii) where paragraph (3) applies, in respect of each of the matters specified in paragraphs 1 and 3 to 7 of Schedule 1.

(3) This paragraph applies where any certificate or information on any matters referred to in paragraph 2 of Schedule 1 is not available to an individual because any provision of the Police Act 1997(**a**) has not been brought into force.

Registered person—general requirements

8.—(1) The registered provider and the registered manager shall, having regard to—

  (a) the size of the fostering agency, its statement of purpose, and the numbers and needs of the children placed by it; and

  (b) the need to safeguard and promote the welfare of the children placed by the fostering agency,

carry on or manage the fostering agency (as the case may be) with sufficient care, competence and skill.

(2) If the registered provider is—

  (a) an individual, he shall undertake;

  (b) an organisation, it shall ensure that the responsible individual undertakes;

  (c) a partnership, it shall ensure that one of the partners undertakes,

  from time to time such training as is appropriate to ensure that he has the experience and skills necessary for carrying on the fostering agency.

(3) The registered manager shall undertake from time to time such training as is appropriate to ensure that he has the experience and skills necessary for managing the fostering agency.

Notification of offences

9. Where the registered person or the responsible individual is convicted of any criminal offence, whether in England and Wales or elsewhere, he shall forthwith give notice in writing to the Commission of—

  (a) the date and place of the conviction;

  (b) the offence of which he was convicted; and

  (c) the penalty imposed on him in respect of the offence.

Local authority fostering service—manager

10.—(1) Each local authority shall appoint one of its officers to manage the local authority fostering service, and shall forthwith notify the Commission of—

  (a) the name of the person appointed; and

  (b) the date on which the appointment is to take effect.

(**a**) *See* footnote to regulation 6(4).

(2) Regulations 7, 8 and 9 shall apply to the manager of a local authority fostering service, in relation to that service, as they apply to the manager of a fostering agency in relation to the fostering agency.

(3) The local authority shall forthwith notify the Commission if the person appointed under paragraph (1) ceases to manage the local authority fostering service.

PART III

CONDUCT OF FOSTERING SERVICES

Independent fostering agencies—duty to secure welfare

11. The registered person in respect of an independent fostering agency(**a**) shall ensure that—
- (a) the welfare of children placed or to be placed with foster parents is safeguarded and promoted at all times; and
- (b) before making any decision affecting a child placed or to be placed with foster parents due consideration is given to—
  - (i) the child's wishes and feelings in the light of his age and understanding; and
  - (ii) his religious persuasion, racial origin and cultural and linguistic background.

Arrangements for the protection of children

12.—(1) The fostering service provider shall prepare and implement a written policy which—
- (a) is intended to safeguard children placed with foster parents from abuse or neglect; and
- (b) sets out the procedure to be followed in the event of any allegation of abuse or neglect.

(2) The procedure under paragraph (1)(b) shall, subject to paragraph (3), provide in particular for—
- (a) liaison and co-operation with any local authority which is, or may be, making child protection enquiries in relation to any child placed by the fostering service provider;
- (b) the prompt referral to the area authority of any allegation of abuse or neglect affecting any child placed by the fostering service provider;
- (c) notification of the instigation and outcome of any child protection enquiries involving a child placed by the fostering service provider, to the Commission;
- (d) written records to be kept of any allegation of abuse or neglect, and of the action taken in response;
- (e) consideration to be given to the measures which may be necessary to protect children placed with foster parents following an allegation of abuse or neglect; and
- (f) arrangements to be made for persons working for the purposes of a fostering service, foster parents and children placed by the fostering service, to have access to information which would enable them to contact—
  - (i) the area authority; and
  - (ii) the Commission,
regarding any concern about child welfare or safety.

(3) Sub-paragraphs (a), (c) and (f)(i) of paragraph (2) do not apply to a local authority fostering service.

(4) In this regulation "child protection enquiries" means any enquiries carried out by a local authority in the exercise of any of its functions conferred by or under the 1989 Act relating to the protection of children.

(**a**) Similar duties already apply to a fostering agency within the meaning of section 4(4)(b) of the 2000 Act by virtue of section 61 of the Children Act 1989, and to a local authority by virtue of section 22 of the Children Act.

Behaviour management and absence from foster parent's home

13.—(1) The fostering service provider shall prepare and implement a written policy on acceptable measures of control, restraint and discipline of children placed with foster parents.

(2) The fostering service provider shall take all reasonable steps to ensure that—

    (a) no form of corporal punishment is used on any child placed with a foster parent;

    (b) no child placed with foster parents is subject to any measure of control, restraint or discipline which is excessive or unreasonable; and

    (c) physical restraint is used on a child only where it is necessary to prevent likely injury to the child or other persons or likely serious damage to property.

(3) The fostering service provider shall prepare and implement a written procedure to be followed if a child is absent from a foster parent's home without permission.

Duty to promote contact

14. The fostering service provider shall, subject to the provisions of the foster placement agreement and any court order relating to contact, promote contact between a child placed with a foster parent and his parents, relatives and friends unless such contact is not reasonably practicable or consistent with the child's welfare.

Health of children placed with foster parents

15.—(1) The fostering service provider shall promote the health and development of children placed with foster parents.

(2) In particular the fostering service provider shall ensure that—

    (a) each child is registered with a general practitioner;

    (b) each child has access to such medical, dental, nursing, psychological and psychiatric advice, treatment and other services as he may require;

    (c) each child is provided with such individual support, aids and equipment which he may require as a result of any particular health needs or disability he may have; and

    (d) each child is provided with guidance, support and advice on health, personal care and health promotion issues appropriate to his needs and wishes.

Education, employment and leisure activities

16.—(1) The fostering service provider shall promote the educational attainment of children placed with foster parents.

(2) In particular the fostering service provider shall—

    (a) establish a procedure for monitoring the educational attainment, progress and school attendance of children placed with foster parents;

    (b) promote the regular school attendance and participation in school activities of school aged children placed with foster parents; and

    (c) provide foster parents with such information and assistance, including equipment, as may be necessary to meet the educational needs of children placed with them.

(3) The fostering service provider shall ensure that any education it provides for any child placed with foster parents who is of compulsory school age but not attending school is efficient and suitable to the child's age, ability, aptitude, and any special educational needs he may have.

(4) The fostering service provider shall ensure that foster parents promote the leisure interests of children placed with them.

(5) Where any child placed with foster parents has attained the age where he is no longer required to receive compulsory full-time education, the fostering service provider shall assist with the making of, and give effect to, the arrangements made for his education, training and employment.

Support, training and information for foster parents

17.—(1) The fostering service provider shall provide foster parents with such training, advice, information and support, including support outside office hours, as appears necessary in the interests of children placed with them.

(2) The fostering service provider shall take all reasonable steps to ensure that foster parents are familiar with, and act in accordance with the policies established in accordance with regulations 12(1) and 13(1) and (3).

(3) The fostering service provider shall ensure that, in relation to any child placed or to be placed with him, a foster parent is given such information, which is kept up to date, as to enable him to provide appropriate care for the child, and in particular that each foster parent is provided with appropriate information regarding—

(a) the state of health and health needs of any child placed or to be placed with him; and

(b) the arrangements for giving consent to the child's medical or dental examination or treatment.

Independent fostering agencies—complaints and representations

18.—(1) Subject to paragraph (7), the registered person in respect of an independent fostering agency(**a**) shall establish a written procedure for considering complaints made by or on behalf of children placed by the agency and foster parents approved by it.

(2) The procedure shall, in particular, provide—

(a) for an opportunity for informal resolution of the complaint at an early stage;

(b) that no person who is the subject of a complaint takes part in its consideration other than, if the registered person considers it appropriate, at the informal resolution stage only;

(c) for dealing with complaints about the registered person;

(d) for complaints to be made by a person acting on behalf of a child;

(e) for arrangements for the procedure to be made known to—

(i) children placed by the agency;

(ii) their parents;

(iii) persons working for the purposes of the independent fostering agency.

(3) A copy of the procedure shall be supplied on request to any of the persons mentioned in paragraph (2)(e).

(4) The copy of the procedure supplied under paragraph (3) shall include—

(a) the name, address and telephone number of the Commission; and

(b) details of the procedure (if any) which has been notified to the registered person by the Commission for the making of complaints to it relating to independent fostering agencies.

(5) The registered person shall ensure that a written record is made of any complaint or representation, the action taken in response to it, and the outcome of the investigation.

(6) The registered person shall ensure that—

(a) children are enabled to make a complaint or representation; and

(b) no child is subject to any reprisal for making a complaint or representation.

(7) The registered person shall supply to the Commission at its request a statement containing a summary of any complaints made during the preceding twelve months and the action taken in response.

(8) This regulation (apart from paragraph (5)) does not apply in relation to any matter to which the Representations Procedure (Children) Regulations 1991(**b**) applies.

Staffing of fostering service

19. The fostering service provider shall ensure that there is, having regard to—

(a) the size of the fostering service, its statement of purpose, and the numbers and needs of the children placed by it; and

---

(**a**) Representations, including complaints, about the discharge of a local authority's functions under Part III of the 1989 Act and about the provision by a voluntary organisation of accommodation to any child who is not looked after by a local authority, are provided for by sections 26(3) to (8), and 59(4) of the 1989 Act, and the Representations Procedure (Children) Regulations 1991 (S.I. 1991/894, as amended by S.I. 1991/2033, S.I. 1993/3069 and S.I. 2001/2874).

(**b**) *See* footnote to regulation 18(1).

(b) the need to safeguard and promote the health and welfare of children placed with foster parents,

a sufficient number of suitably qualified, competent and experienced persons working for purposes of the fostering service.

Fitness of workers

20.—(1) The fostering service provider shall not—

(a) employ a person to work for the purposes of the fostering service unless that person is fit to work for the purposes of a fostering service; or

(b) allow a person to whom paragraph (2) applies, to work for the purposes of the fostering service unless that person is fit to work for the purposes of a fostering service.

(2) This paragraph applies to any person who is employed by a person other than the fostering service provider in a position in which he may in the course of his duties have regular contact with children placed by the fostering service.

(3) For the purposes of paragraph (1), a person is not fit to work for the purposes of a fostering service unless—

(a) he is of integrity and good character;

(b) he has the qualifications, skills and experience necessary for the work he is to perform;

(c) he is physically and mentally fit for the work he is to perform; and

(d) full and satisfactory information is available in relation to him in respect of the following matters—

(i) except where paragraph (4) applies, each of the matters specified in paragraphs 1 to 6 of Schedule 1;

(ii) where paragraph (4) applies, each of the matters specified in paragraphs 1 and 3 to 7 of Schedule 1.

(4) This paragraph applies where any certificate or information on any matters referred to in paragraph 2 of Schedule 1 is not available to an individual because any provision of the Police Act 1997(**a**) has not been brought into force.

(5) The fostering service provider shall take reasonable steps to ensure that any person working for a fostering service who is not employed by him and to whom paragraph (2) does not apply, is appropriately supervised while carrying out his duties.

(6) Subject to regulation 50(7), the fostering service provider shall not employ to work for the purposes of the fostering service in a position to which paragraph (7) applies, a person who is—

(a) a foster parent approved by the fostering service; or

(b) a member of the household of such a foster parent.

(7) This paragraph applies to any management, social work or other professional position, unless in the case of a position which is not a management or a social work position, the work is undertaken on an occasional basis, as a volunteer, or for no more than 5 hours in any week.

Employment of staff

21.—(1) The fostering service provider shall—

(a) ensure that all permanent appointments are subject to the satisfactory completion of a period of probation; and

(b) provide all employees with a job description outlining their responsibilities.

(2) The fostering service provider shall operate a disciplinary procedure which, in particular—

(a) provides for the suspension of an employee where necessary in the interests of the safety or welfare of children placed with foster parents;

(b) provides that the failure on the part of an employee to report an incident of abuse, or suspected abuse of a child placed with foster parents to an appropriate person is a ground on which disciplinary proceedings may be instituted.

(**a**) *See* footnote to regulation 6(4).

(3) For the purposes of paragraph (2)(b), an appropriate person is—

    (a) in any case—

        (i) the registered person, or the manager of the local authority fostering service as the case may be;

        (ii) an officer of the Commission;

        (iii) an officer of the area authority if applicable;

        (iv) a police officer;

        (v) an officer of the National Society for the Prevention of Cruelty to Children;

    (b) in the case of an employee of an independent fostering agency, an officer of the responsible authority;

    (c) in the case of an employee of a fostering agency, an officer of the local authority in whose area the agency is situated.

(4) The fostering service provider shall ensure that all persons employed by him—

    (a) receive appropriate training, supervision and appraisal; and

    (b) are enabled from to time to time to obtain further qualifications appropriate to the work they perform.

Records with respect to fostering services

22.—(1) The fostering service provider shall maintain and keep up to date the records specified in Schedule 2.

(2) The records referred to in paragraph (1) shall be retained for at least 15 years from the date of the last entry.

Fitness of premises

23.—(1) The fostering service provider shall not use premises for the purposes of a fostering service unless the premises are suitable for the purpose of achieving the aims and objectives set out in the statement of purpose.

(2) A fostering service provider shall ensure—

    (a) that there are adequate security arrangements at the premises, in particular that there are secure facilities for the storage of records; and

    (b) that any records which are stored away from the premises are kept in conditions of appropriate security.

PART IV

APPROVAL OF FOSTER PARENTS

Establishment of fostering panel

24.—(1) Subject to paragraph (5), the fostering service provider shall establish at least one panel, to be known as a fostering panel, in accordance with this regulation.

(2) The fostering service provider shall appoint to chair the panel either—

    (a) a senior member of staff of the fostering service provider who is not responsible for the day to day management of any person carrying out assessments of prospective foster parents; or

    (b) such other person not being an employee, member, partner or director of the fostering service provider, who has the skills and experience necessary for chairing a fostering panel.

(3) Subject to paragraph (5), the fostering panel shall consist of no more than 10 members including the person appointed under paragraph (2) and shall include—

    (a) two social workers employed by the fostering service provider, one of whom has child care expertise and the other of whom has expertise in the provision of a fostering service;

    (b) in the case of a fostering agency—

(i) if the registered provider is an individual, that individual;

(ii) if the registered provider is an organisation, at least one of its directors or the responsible individual;

(iii) if the registered provider is a partnership, at least one of the partners;

(c) in the case of a local authority fostering service, at least one elected member of the local authority; and

(d) at least four other persons (in this regulation referred to as "independent members"), including at least one person who is, or within the previous two years has been, a foster parent for a fostering service provider other than the one whose fostering panel is being established.

(4) The fostering service provider shall appoint a member of the fostering panel who will act as chair if the person appointed to chair the panel is absent or his office is vacant ("the vice chair").

(5) A fostering panel may be established jointly by any two but not more than three fostering service providers, and if such a fostering panel is established—

(a) the maximum number of members who may be appointed to that panel is eleven;

(b) each fostering service provider shall appoint two persons to the panel, one of whom falls within paragraph (3)(a), and the other of whom falls within paragraph (3)(b) or (c), as the case may be;

(c) by agreement between the fostering service providers there shall be appointed—

(i) a person to chair the panel;

(ii) at least four independent members including at least one person who is, or within the previous two years has been, a foster parent for a fostering service provider other than any of those whose fostering panel is being established; and

(iii) a member of the panel who will act as chair if the person appointed to chair the panel is absent or his office is vacant ("the vice chair").

(6) A fostering panel member shall hold office for a term not exceeding three years, and may not hold office for the panel of the same fostering service provider for more than two consecutive terms.

(7) Any panel member may resign his office at any time by giving one month's notice in writing to the fostering service provider.

(8) Where a fostering service provider is of the opinion that any member of the fostering panel is unsuitable or unable to remain in office, it may terminate his office at any time by giving him notice in writing.

(9) A person shall not be appointed as an independent member of a fostering panel if—

(a) he is a foster parent approved by the fostering service provider;

(b) he is employed by the fostering service provider;

(c) he is concerned in the management of the fostering service provider;

(d) in the case of a local authority fostering service, he is an elected member of the local authority; or

(e) in the case of a fostering agency, he is related to an employee of the registered provider, or to any person concerned in the management of the fostering agency.

(10) For the purposes of paragraph (9)(e), a person ("person A") is related to another person ("person B") if he is—

(a) a member of the household of, or married to person B;

(b) the son, daughter, mother, father, sister or brother of person B; or

(c) the son, daughter, mother, father, sister or brother of the person to whom person B is married.

Meetings of fostering panel

25.—(1) Subject to paragraph (3), no business shall be conducted by a fostering panel unless at least five of its members, including the person appointed to chair the panel, or the vice chair, at least one of the social workers employed by the fostering service and at least two of the independent members, meet as a panel.

(2) A fostering panel shall make a written record of its proceedings and the reasons for its recommendations.

(3) In the case of a joint fostering panel, no business shall be conducted unless at least six of its members, including the person appointed to chair the panel, or the vice chair, and one social worker from each fostering service, meet as a panel.

Functions of fostering panel

26.—(1) The functions of the fostering panel in respect of cases referred to it by the fostering service provider are—

    (a) to consider each application for approval and to recommend whether or not a person is suitable to act as a foster parent;

    (b) where it recommends approval of an application, to recommend the terms on which the approval is to be given;

    (c) to recommend whether or not a person remains suitable to act as a foster parent, and whether or not the terms of his approval remain appropriate—

        (i) on the first review carried out in accordance with regulation 29(1); and

        (ii) on the occasion of any other review when requested to do so by the fostering service provider in accordance with regulation 29(5); and

    (d) to consider any case referred to it under regulation 28(8) or 29(9).

(2) The fostering panel shall also—

    (a) advise on the procedures under which reviews in accordance with regulation 29 are carried out by the fostering service provider and periodically monitor their effectiveness;

    (b) oversee the conduct of assessments carried out by the fostering service provider; and

    (c) give advice and make recommendations on such other matters or cases as the fostering service provider may refer to it.

(3) In this regulation "recommend" means recommend to the fostering service provider.

Assessment of prospective foster parents

27.—(1) The fostering service provider shall carry out an assessment of any person whom it considers may be suitable to become a foster parent, in accordance with this regulation.

(2) If the fostering service provider considers that a person may be suitable to act as a foster parent it shall—

    (a) obtain the information specified in Schedule 3 relating to the prospective foster parent and other members of his household and family, and any other information it considers relevant;

    (b) interview at least two persons nominated by the prospective foster parent to provide personal references for him, and prepare written reports of the interviews;

    (c) subject to paragraph (3), consult with, and take into account the views of, the local authority in whose area the prospective foster parent lives;

    (d) having regard to these matters consider whether the prospective foster parent is suitable to act as a foster parent and whether his household is suitable for any child in respect of whom approval may be given;

    (e) prepare a written report on him which includes the matters set out in paragraph (4); and

    (f) refer the report to the fostering panel and notify the prospective foster parent accordingly.

(3) Paragraph (2)(c) does not apply where the fostering service provider is a local authority and the applicant lives in the area of that authority.

[14]

(4) The report referred to in paragraph (2)(e) shall include the following matters in relation to the prospective foster parent—

(a) the information required by Schedule 3 and any other information the fostering service provider considers relevant;

(b) the fostering service provider's assessment of his suitability to act as a foster parent; and

(c) the fostering service provider's proposals about the terms and conditions of any approval.

(5) Subject to paragraph (6), a person shall not be regarded as suitable to act as a foster parent if he or any member of his household aged 18 or over—

(a) has been convicted of a specified offence committed at the age of 18 or over; or

(b) has been cautioned by a constable in respect of any such offence which, at the time the caution was given, he admitted.

(6) The fostering service provider may regard a person to whom paragraph (5) would, apart from this paragraph apply, as suitable to act or to continue to act, as the case may be, as a foster parent in relation to a particular named child or children if the fostering service provider is satisfied that the welfare of that child or those children requires it, and either—

(a) the person, or a member of his household, is a relative of the child; or

(b) the person is already acting as a foster parent for the child.

(7) In this regulation "specified offence" means—

(a) an offence against a child;

(b) an offence specified in Schedule 4;

(c) an offence contrary to section 170 of the Customs and Excise Management Act 1979(a) in relation to goods prohibited to be imported under section 42 of the Customs Consolidation Act 1876 (prohibitions and restrictions relating to pornography)(b) where the prohibited goods included indecent photographs of children under the age of 16;

(d) any other offence involving bodily injury to a child or young person, other than an offence of common assault or battery, and

the expression "offence against a child" has the meaning given to it by section 26(1) of the Criminal Justice and Court Services Act 2000(c) except that it does not include an offence contrary to sections 6, 12 or 13 of the Sexual Offences Act 1956 (sexual intercourse with a girl aged 13 to 16, buggery, or indecency between men)(d) in a case where the offender was under the age of 20 at the time the offence was committed.

Approval of foster parents

28.—(1) A fostering service provider shall not approve a person who has been approved as a foster parent by another fostering service provider, and whose approval has not been terminated.

(2) A fostering service provider shall not approve a person as a foster parent unless—

(a) it has completed its assessment of his suitability; and

(b) its fostering panel has considered the application.

(3) A fostering service provider shall in deciding whether to approve a person as a foster parent and as to the terms of any approval, take into account the recommendation of its fostering panel.

(4) No member of its fostering panel shall take part in any decision made by a fostering service provider under paragraph (3).

(5) If a fostering service provider decides to approve a person as a foster parent it shall—

(a) give him notice in writing specifying the terms of the approval, for example, whether

(a) 1979 c. 2.
(b) 1876 c. 36.
(c) 2000 c. 43.
(d) 1956 c. 69.

it is in respect of a particular named child or children, or number and age range of children, or of placements of any particular kind, or in any particular circumstances; and

(b) enter into a written agreement with him covering the matters specified in Schedule 5 (in these Regulations referred to as the "foster care agreement").

(6) If a fostering service provider considers that a person is not suitable to act as a foster parent it shall—

(a) given him written notice that it proposes not to approve him, together with its reasons and a copy of the fostering panel's recommendation; and

(b) invite him to submit any written representations within 28 days of the date of the notice.

(7) If the fostering service provider does not receive any representations within the period referred to in paragraph (6)(b), it may proceed to make its decision.

(8) If the fostering service provider receives any written representations within the period referred to in paragraph (6)(b), it shall—

(a) refer the case to the fostering panel for further consideration; and

(b) make its decision, taking into account any fresh recommendation made by the fostering panel.

(9) As soon as practicable after making the decision referred to in paragraph (7) or (8)(b) as the case may be, the fostering service provider shall notify the prospective foster parent in writing and—

(a) if the decision is to approve the person as a foster parent, comply with paragraph (5) in relation to him; or

(b) if the decision is not to approve the person, provide written reasons for its decision.

Reviews and terminations of approval

29.—(1) The fostering service provider shall review the approval of each foster parent in accordance with this regulation.

(2) A review shall take place not more that a year after approval, and thereafter whenever the fostering service provider considers it necessary, but at intervals of not more than a year.

(3) When undertaking a review, the fostering service provider shall—

(a) make such enquiries and obtain such information as it considers necessary in order to review whether the person continues to be suitable as to act as a foster parent and his household continues to be suitable; and

(b) seek and take into account the views of—

(i) the foster parent;

(ii) (subject to the child's age and understanding) any child placed with the foster parent; and

(iii) any responsible authority which has within the preceding year placed a child with the foster parent.

(4) At the conclusion of the review the fostering service provider shall prepare a written report, setting out whether—

(a) the person continues to be suitable to act as a foster parent and his household continues to be suitable; and

(b) the terms of his approval continue to be appropriate.

(5) The fostering service provider shall on the occasion of the first review under this regulation, and may on any subsequent review, refer its report to the fostering panel for consideration.

(6) If the fostering service provider decides, taking into account any recommendation made by the fostering panel, that the foster parent and his household continue to be suitable and that the terms of his approval continue to be appropriate, it shall give written notice to the foster parent of its decision.

[16]

(7) If, taking into account any recommendation made by the fostering panel, the fostering service provider is no longer satisfied that the foster parent and his household continue to be suitable, or that the terms of the approval are appropriate, it shall—

(a) give written notice to the foster parent that it proposes to terminate, or revise the terms of, his approval as the case may be, together with its reasons, and

(b) invite him to submit any written representations within 28 days of the date of the notice.

(8) If the fostering service provider does not receive any representations within the period referred to in paragraph (7)(b), it may proceed to make its decision.

(9) If the fostering service provider receives any written representations within the period referred to in paragraph (7)(b), it shall—

(a) refer the case to the fostering panel for its consideration; and

(b) make its decision, taking into account any recommendation made by the fostering panel.

(10) As soon as practicable after making the decision referred to in paragraph (8) or (9)(b), the fostering service provider shall give written notice to the foster parent stating, as the case may be—

(a) that the foster parent and his household continue to be suitable, and that the terms of the approval continue to be appropriate;

(b) that his approval is terminated from a specified date, and the reasons for the termination; or

(c) the revised terms of the approval and the reasons for the revision.

(11) A foster parent may give notice in writing to the fostering service provider at any time that he no longer wishes to act as a foster parent, whereupon his approval is terminated with effect from 28 days from the date on which the notice is received by the fostering service provider.

(12) A copy of any notice given under this regulation shall be sent to the responsible authority for any child placed with the foster parent (unless the responsible authority is also the fostering service provider), and the area authority.

Case records relating to foster parents and others

30.—(1) A fostering service provider shall maintain a case record for each foster parent approved by it which shall include copies of the documents specified in paragraph (2) and the information specified in paragraph (3).

(2) The documents referred to in paragraph (1) are, as the case may be—

(a) the notice of approval given under regulation 28(5)(a);

(b) the foster care agreement;

(c) any report of a review of approval prepared under regulation 29(4);

(d) any notice given under regulation 29(10);

(e) any agreement entered into in accordance with regulation 38(1)(a);

(f) the report prepared under regulation 27(2)(e) and any other reports submitted to the fostering panel; and

(g) any recommendations made by the fostering panel.

(3) The information referred to in paragraph (1) is, as the case may be—

(a) a record of each placement with the foster parent, including the name, age and sex of each child placed, the dates on which each placement began and terminated and the circumstances of the termination;

(b) the information obtained by the fostering service provider in relation to the assessment and approval of the foster parent and in relation to any review or termination of the approval.

(4) A local authority shall maintain a case record for each person with whom a child is placed under regulation 38(2) which shall include in relation to that person—

(a) the agreement entered into in accordance with regulation 38(2)(b);

  (b) a record in relation to the placement, including the name, age and sex of each child placed, the dates on which the placement began and terminated, and the circumstances of the termination; and

  (c) the information obtained in relation to the enquiries carried out under regulation 38(2).

(5) The fostering service provider shall compile a record for each person whom it does not approve as a foster parent, or who withdraws his application prior to approval, which shall included in relation to him—

  (a) the information obtained in connection with the assessment;

  (b) any report submitted to the fostering panel and any recommendation made by the fostering panel; and

  (c) any notification given under regulation 28.

Register of foster parents

31.—(1) The fostering service provider shall enter, in a register kept for the purpose, the particulars specified in paragraph (2) and in the case of a local authority fostering service, it shall also enter the particulars specified in paragraph (3).

(2) The particulars are—

  (a) the name, address, date of birth and sex of each foster parent;

  (b) the date of his approval and of each review of his approval; and

  (c) the current terms of his approval.

(3) Each local authority shall enter in its register—

  (a) the name and address of each person with whom it has placed a child under regulation 38(2);

  (b) the date of each agreement entered into in accordance with regulation 38(2)(b); and

  (c) the terms of any such agreement for the time being in force.

Retention and confidentiality of records

32.—(1) The records compiled in relation to a foster parent under regulation 30(1), and any entry relating to him in the register maintained under regulation 31(1) shall be retained for at least 10 years from the date on which his approval is terminated.

(2) The records compiled by a local authority under regulation 30(4) in relation to a person with whom a child is placed under regulation 38(2), and any entry relating to such a person in the register maintained under regulation 31(1), shall be retained for at least 10 years from the date on which the placement is terminated.

(3) The records compiled under regulation 30(5) shall be retained for at least 3 years from the refusal or withdrawal, as the case may be, of the application to become a foster parent.

(4) The requirement in paragraphs (1) to (3) may be complied with by retaining the original written records or copies of them, or by keeping all or part of the information contained in them in some other accessible form such as a computer record.

(5) Any records or register maintained in accordance with regulation 30 or 31 shall be kept securely and may not be disclosed to any person except in accordance with—

  (a) any provision of, or made under, or by virtue of, a statute under which access to such records is authorised;

  (b) any court order authorising access to such records.

PART V

PLACEMENTS

General duty of responsible authority

33. A responsible authority shall not place a child with a foster parent unless it is satisfied that—

    (a) it is the most suitable way of performing its duty under (as the case may be) section 22(3) or 61(1)(a) and (b) of the 1989 Act; and

    (b) a placement with the particular foster parent is the most suitable placement having regard to all the circumstances.

Making of placements

34.—(1) Except in the case of an emergency or immediate placement under regulation 38, a responsible authority may only place a child with a foster parent if—

    (a) the foster parent is approved—

        (i) by the responsible authority proposing to make the placement; or

        (ii) provided the conditions specified in paragraph (2) are satisfied, by another fostering service provider;

    (b) the terms of his approval are consistent with the proposed placement; and

    (c) he has entered into a foster care agreement.

(2) The conditions referred to in paragraph (1)(a)(ii) are—

    (a) that the fostering service provider by whom the foster parent is approved, consents to the placement;

    (b) that any other responsible authority which already has a child placed with the foster parent, consents to the placement;

    (c) where applicable, that the area authority is consulted, its views are taken into account, and it is given notice if the placement is made; and

    (d) where the foster parent is approved by an independent fostering agency, the requirements of regulation 40 are complied with.

(3) Before making a placement, the responsible authority shall enter into a written agreement (in these regulations referred to as the "foster placement agreement") with the foster parent relating to the child, which covers the matters specified in Schedule 6.

Supervision of placements

35.—(1) A responsible authority shall satisfy itself that the welfare of each child placed by it continues to be suitably provided for by the placement, and for that purpose the authority shall make arrangements for a person authorised by the authority to visit the child, in the home in which he is placed—

    (a) from time to time as circumstances may require;

    (b) when reasonably requested by the child or the foster parent; and

    (c) in any event (subject to regulation 37)—

        (i) in the first year of the placement, within one week from its beginning and then at intervals of not more than six weeks;

        (ii) subsequently, at intervals of not more than 3 months.

(2) In the case of an immediate placement under regulation 38, the local authority shall arrange for the child to be visited at least once in each week during the placement.

(3) On each occasion on which the child is visited under this regulation the responsible authority shall ensure that the person it has authorised to carry out the visit—

    (a) sees the child alone unless the child, being of sufficient age and understanding to do so, refuses; and

    (b) prepares a written report of the visit.

Termination of placements

36.—(1) A responsible authority shall not allow the placement of a child with a particular person to continue if it appears to them that the placement is no longer the most suitable way of performing their duty under (as the case may be) section 22(3) or 61(1)(a) and (b) of the Act.

(2) Where it appears to an area authority that the continuation of a placement would be detrimental to the welfare of the child concerned, the area authority shall remove the child forthwith.

(3) An area authority which removes a child under paragraph (2) shall forthwith notify the responsible authority.

Short-term placements

37.—(1) This regulation applies where a responsible authority has arranged to place a child in a series of short-term placements with the same foster parent and the arrangement is such that—

> (a) no single placement is to last for more than four weeks; and
>
> (b) the total duration of the placements is not to exceed 120 days in any period of 12 months.

(2) A series of short-term placements to which this regulation applies may be treated as a single placement for the purposes of these Regulations, but with the modifications set out in paragraphs (3) and (4).

(3) Regulation 35(1)(c)(i) and (ii) shall apply as if they required arrangements to be made for visits to the child on a day when he is in fact placed ("a placement day")—

> (a) within the first seven placement days of a series of short-term placements; and
>
> (b) thereafter, if the series of placements continues, at intervals of not more than six months or, if the interval between placements exceeds six months, during the next placement.

(4) Regulation 41 shall apply as if it required arrangements to be made for visits to the child on a placement day within the first seven placement days of a series of short-term placements.

Emergency and immediate placements by local authorities

38.—(1) Where a child is to be placed in an emergency, a local authority may for a period not exceeding 24 hours place the child with any foster parent approved by the local authority or any other fostering service provider provided that—

> (a) the foster parent has made a written agreement with the local authority to carry out the duties specified in paragraph (3); and
>
> (b) the local authority are satisfied as to the provisions of regulation 33(a).

(2) Where a local authority are satisfied that the immediate placement of a child is necessary, they may place the child with a person who is not a foster parent after interviewing him, inspecting the accommodation and obtaining information about other persons living in his household, for a period not exceeding six weeks, provided that—

> (a) the person is a relative or friend of the child;
>
> (b) the person has made a written agreement with the local authority to carry out the duties specified in paragraph (3); and
>
> (c) the local authority are satisfied as to the provisions of regulation 33(a).

(3) The duties referred to in paragraphs (1)(a) and (2)(b) are—

> (a) to care for the child as if he were a member of that person's family;
>
> (b) to permit any person authorised by the local authority or (if applicable) the area authority, to visit the child at any time;
>
> (c) where regulation 36 applies, to allow the child to be removed at any time by the local authority or (if applicable) the area authority;
>
> (d) to ensure that any information which that person may acquire relating to the child, his family or any other person, which has been given to him in confidence in connection with the placement is kept confidential and is not disclosed except to, or with the agreement of, the local authority; and

[20]

(e) to allow contact with the child in accordance with the terms of any court order relating to contact or any arrangements made or agreed by the local authority.

(4) Where a local authority make a placement under this regulation outside their area they shall notify the area authority.

Placements outside England

39.—(1) A voluntary organisation shall not place a child outside the British Islands(**a**).

(2) Where a responsible authority makes arrangements to place a child outside England it shall ensure, so far as reasonably practicable, that the requirements which would have applied under these Regulations had the child been placed in England, are complied with.

(3) In the case of a placement by a local authority outside England or Wales, paragraph (2) is subject to the provisions of paragraph 19 of Schedule 2 to the 1989 Act (arrangements to assist children to live abroad).

Independent fostering agencies—discharge of local authority functions

40.—(1) A local authority may make arrangements in accordance with this regulation for the duties imposed on it as a responsible authority by regulations 34, 35, 36(1) and 37 and where paragraph (3) applies, 33(b) to be discharged on its behalf by a registered person.

(2) Subject to paragraph (3), no arrangements may be made under this regulation in respect of a particular child, unless a local authority has performed its duties under regulation 33 in relation to that child.

(3) Where a local authority makes arrangements with a registered person for the registered person to provide foster parents for the purposes of a short-term placement within the meaning of regulation 37(1), the local authority may also make arrangements for the registered person to perform the local authority's duty under regulation 33(b) in relation to that placement on its behalf.

(4) No arrangements may be made under this regulation unless a local authority has entered into a written agreement with the registered person which sets out—

(a) which of its duties the local authority proposes to delegate in accordance with this regulation;

(b) the services to be provided to the local authority by the registered person;

(c) the arrangements for the selection by the local authority of particular foster parents from those approved by the registered person;

(d) a requirement for the registered person to submit reports to the local authority on any placement as may be required by the authority, and in particular following any visit carried out under regulation 35; and

(e) the arrangements for the termination of the agreement.

(5) Where a local authority proposes to make an arrangement under this regulation in respect of a particular child the local authority shall enter into an agreement with the registered person in respect of that child which sets out—

(a) details of the particular foster parent with whom the child is to be placed;

(b) details of any services the child is to receive;

(c) the terms (including as to payment) of the proposed foster placement agreement;

(d) the arrangements for record keeping about the child, and for the return of records at the end of the placement;

(e) a requirement for the registered person to notify the local authority immediately in the event of any concerns about the placement; and

(f) whether and on what basis other children may be placed with the foster parent.

(**a**) "British Islands" are defined in the Interpretation Act 1978 (c. 30) as meaning the United Kingdom, the Channel Islands and the Isle of Man.

(6) A foster parent with whom a child is placed in accordance with arrangements made under this regulation is, in relation to that placement, to be treated for the purposes of paragraph 12(d) of Schedule 2 to the 1989 Act as a local authority foster parent.

(7) A local authority shall report to the Commission any concerns it may have about the services provided by a registered person.

(8) In this regulation "registered person" means a person who is the registered person in respect of an independent fostering agency.

PART VI

LOCAL AUTHORITY VISITS

Local authority visits to children placed by voluntary organisations

41.—(1) Every local authority shall arrange for a person authorised by the local authority to visit every child who is placed with a foster parent within their area by a voluntary organisation as follows—

(a) subject to regulation 37(4), within 28 days of the placement;

(b) within 14 days of receipt of a request from the voluntary organisation which made the placement to visit a child;

(c) as soon as reasonably practicable if it is informed that the welfare of the child may not be being safeguarded or promoted; and

(d) at intervals of not more than six months where the local authority are satisfied, following a visit to a child under this regulation that the child's welfare is being safeguarded and promoted.

(2) Every local authority shall ensure that a person carrying out a visit in accordance with paragraph (1)—

(a) sees the child during the course of the visit, or if the child is not there, makes arrangements to see the child as soon as reasonably practicable; and

(b) takes steps to discover whether the voluntary organisation which placed the child have made suitable arrangements to perform their duties under these Regulations, and those under section 61 of the 1989 Act.

(3) A local authority shall report to the Commission any concerns it may have about the voluntary organisation.

PART VII

FOSTERING AGENCIES—MISCELLANEOUS

Review of quality of care

42.—(1) The registered person shall establish and maintain a system for—

(a) monitoring the matters set out in Schedule 7 at appropriate intervals; and

(b) improving the quality of foster care provided by the fostering agency.

(2) The registered person shall supply to the Commission a report in respect of any review conducted by him for the purposes of paragraph (1) and make a copy of the report available upon request to the persons mentioned in regulation 3(2).

(3) The system referred to in paragraph (1) shall provide for consultation with foster parents, children placed with foster parents, and their responsible authority (unless, in the case of a fostering agency which is a voluntary organisation, it is also the responsible authority).

Notifiable events

43.—(1) If, in relation to a fostering agency, any of the events listed in column 1 of the table in Schedule 8 takes place, the registered person shall without delay notify the persons indicated in respect of the event in column 2 of the table.

(2) Any notification made in accordance with this regulation which is given orally shall be confirmed in writing.

Financial position

44.—(1) The registered provider shall carry on the fostering agency in such manner as is likely to ensure that it will be financially viable for the purpose of achieving the aims and objectives set out in its statement of purpose.

(2) The registered provider shall—

    (a) ensure that adequate accounts are maintained and kept up to date in respect of the fostering agency; and

    (b) supply a copy of the accounts, certified by an accountant to the Commission.

(3) The registered provider shall, if the Commission so requests, provide the Commission with such information as it may require for the purpose of considering the financial viability of the fostering agency, including—

    (a) the annual accounts of the fostering agency, certified by an accountant;

    (b) a reference from a bank expressing an opinion as to the registered provider's financial standing;

    (c) information as to the financing and financial resources of the fostering agency;

    (d) where the registered provider is a company, information as to any of its associated companies; and

    (e) a certificate of insurance for the registered provider in respect of liability which may be incurred by him in relation to the fostering agency in respect of death, injury, public liability, damage or other loss.

(4) In this regulation one company is associated with another if one of them has control of the other, or both are under the control of the same person.

Notice of absence

45.—(1) Where the registered manager proposes to be absent from the fostering agency for a continuous period of 28 days or more, the registered person shall give notice in writing to the Commission of the proposed absence.

(2) Except in the case of an emergency, the notice referred to in paragraph (1) shall be given no later than one month before the proposed absence is to start, or within such shorter period as may be agreed with the Commission, and the notice shall specify—

    (a) the length or expected length of the proposed absence;

    (b) the reason for the proposed absence;

    (c) the arrangements which have been made for the running of the fostering agency during that absence;

    (d) the name, address and qualifications of the person who will be responsible for the fostering agency during the absence; and

    (e) the arrangements that have been made or are proposed to be made for appointing another person to manage the fostering agency during the absence, including the proposed date by which the appointment is to start.

(3) Where the absence arises as a result of an emergency, the registered person shall give notice of the absence within one week of its occurrence, specifying the matters mentioned in sub-paragraphs (a) to (e) of paragraph (2).

(4) Where the registered manager has been absent from the fostering agency for a continuous period of 28 days or more, and the Commission has not been given notice of the absence, the registered person shall without delay give notice in writing to the Commission specifying the matters mentioned in paragraph (2).

(5) The registered person shall notify the Commission of the return to duty of the registered manager not later than 7 days after the date of his return.

Notice of changes

46.—(1) The registered person shall give notice in writing to the Commission as soon as it is practicable to do so if any of the following events takes place or is proposed to take place—

  (a) a person other than the registered person carries on or manages the fostering agency;

  (b) a person ceases to carry on or manage the fostering agency;

  (c) where the registered provider is an individual, he changes his name;

  (d) where the registered provider is a partnership, there is any change in the membership of the partnership;

  (e) where the registered provider is an organisation—

      (i) the name or address of the organisation is changed;

      (ii) there is any change of director, manager, secretary or other similar officer of the organisation;

      (iii) there is to be any change in the identity of the responsible individual;

  (f) where the registered provider is an individual, a trustee in bankruptcy is appointed or he makes any composition or arrangement with his creditors; or

  (g) where the registered provider is a company, or a partnership, a receiver, manager, liquidator or provisional liquidator is appointed in respect of the registered provider.

(2) The registered provider shall notify the Commission in writing and without delay of the death of the registered manager.

Appointment of liquidators etc.

47.—(1) Any person to whom paragraph (2) applies shall—

  (a) forthwith notify the Commission of his appointment indicating the reasons for it;

  (b) appoint a manager to take full-time day to day charge of the fostering agency in any case where there is no registered manager; and

  (c) not more than 28 days after his appointment notify the Commission of his intentions regarding the future operation of the fostering agency.

(2) This paragraph applies to any person appointed as—

  (a) the receiver or manager of the property of a company or partnership which is a registered provider of a fostering agency;

  (b) a liquidator or provisional liquidator of a company which is the registered provider of a fostering agency; or

  (c) the trustee in bankruptcy of a registered provider of a fostering agency.

Offences

48.—(1) A contravention or failure to comply with any of the provisions of regulations 3 to 23 and 42 to 46 shall be an offence.

(2) The Commission shall not bring proceedings against a person in respect of any contravention or failure to comply with those regulations unless—

  (a) subject to paragraph 4, he is a registered person;

  (b) notice has been given to him in accordance with paragraph (3);

  (c) the period specified in the notice has expired;

  (d) the registered person contravenes or fails to comply with any of the provisions of the regulations mentioned in the notice.

(3) Where the Commission considers that the registered person has contravened or failed to comply with any of the provisions of the regulations mentioned in paragraph (1), it may serve a notice on the registered person specifying—

  (a) in what respect in its opinion the registered person has contravened or is contravening any of the regulations, or has failed or is failing to comply with the requirements of any of the regulations;

  (b) what action, in the opinion of the Commission, the registered person should take so as to comply with any of those regulations; and

  (c) the period, not exceeding three months, within which the registered person should take action.

(4) The Commission may bring proceedings against a person who was once, but no longer is, a registered person, in respect of a failure to comply with regulation 22 or 32, and for this purpose, references in paragraphs (2) and (3) to a registered person shall be taken to include such a person.

Compliance with regulations

49. Where there is more than one registered person in respect of a fostering agency, anything which is required under these Regulations to be done by the registered person shall, if done by one of the registered persons, not be required to be done by any of the other registered persons.

PART VIII

MISCELLANEOUS

Transitional provisions

50.—(1) This paragraph applies to a fostering agency falling within section 4(4)(b) of the 2000 Act (a voluntary organisation which places children with foster parents under section 59(1) of the 1989 Act) which has, before the coming into force of these Regulations duly made an application for registration under Part II of the 2000 Act.

(2) These Regulations shall apply to a fostering agency to which paragraph (1) applies, as if any reference in them to a registered person is a reference to the person who carries on the agency(**a**)—

(a) until such time as the application for registration is granted, either unconditionally or subject only to conditions which have been agreed in writing between that person and the Commission; or

(b) if the application is granted subject to conditions which have not been so agreed, or it is refused—

(i) if no appeal is brought, until the expiration of the period of 28 days after service on that person of notice of the Commission's decision; or

(ii) if an appeal is brought, until it is determined or abandoned.

(3) This paragraph applies to an independent fostering agency which is carried on by a voluntary organisation, which has, before the coming into force of these Regulations, duly made an application for registration under Part II of the 2000 Act.

(4) Where a local authority looking after a child is satisfied that the child should be placed with foster parents, they may make arrangements, subject to paragraph (5), for the duties imposed on them by regulations 34, 35, 36(1) and 37 to be discharged on their behalf by the voluntary organisation to which paragraph (3) applies ("an unregistered independent voluntary provider")—

(a) until such time as the application for registration is granted, either unconditionally or subject only to conditions which have been agreed in writing between that provider and the Commission; or

(b) if the application is granted subject to conditions which have not been so agreed, or it is refused—

(i) if no appeal is brought, until the expiration of the period of 28 days after service on that provider of notice of the Commission's decision; or

(ii) if an appeal is brought, until it is determined or abandoned.

(5) A local authority may not make arrangements under paragraph (4) unless they—

(a) are satisfied—

(i) as to the capacity of the unregistered independent voluntary provider to discharge duties on their behalf; and

(ii) that those arrangements are the most suitable way for those duties to be discharged; and

(**a**) *See* Section 121(4) of the Care Standards Act 2000.

(b) enter into a written agreement with the unregistered independent voluntary provider about the arrangements, providing for consultation and exchange of information and reports between the local authority and the unregistered independent voluntary agency.

(6) Paragraphs (2) and (4) are subject to the provisions of Article 2 of, and sub-paragraphs (5) and (6) of paragraph 15 of Schedule 1 to, the Care Standards Act 2000 (Commencement No. 9 (England) and Transitional Provisions) Order 2001 (application by the Commission to a justice of the peace)(**a**).

(7) Regulation 20(6) shall not apply to any person to whom it would, apart from this regulation apply, if he is on 1st April 2002 already employed by a fostering service provider in a position to which paragraph (7) of that regulation applies.

Revocation

51.   The following Regulations are revoked—

(a) the Foster Placement (Children) Regulations 1991(**b**);

(b) regulation 2 of the Children (Short-term Placements) (Miscellaneous Amendments) Regulations 1995(**c**);

(c) regulation 3 of the Children (Protection from Offenders) (Miscellaneous Amendments) Regulations 1997(**d**);

(d) regulation 2 of the Children (Protection from Offenders) (Amendment) Regulations 1999(**e**) so far as it amends the Foster Placement (Children) Regulations 1991; and

(e) regulation 2 of the Foster Placement (Children) and Adoption Agencies Amendment (England) Regulations 2001(**f**).

Signed by authority of the Secretary of State for Health

Jacqui Smith
Minister of State,
Department of Health

14th January 2002

(**a**) S.I. 2001/3852 (c. 125).
(**b**) S.I. 1991/910.
(**c**) S.I. 1995/2015.
(**d**) S.I. 1997/2308.
(**e**) S.I. 1999/2768.
(**f**) S.I. 2001/2992.

SCHEDULE 1   Regulations 5, 7, 20

INFORMATION REQUIRED IN RESPECT OF PERSONS SEEKING TO CARRY ON, MANAGE OR WORK FOR THE PURPOSES OF A FOSTERING SERVICE

1. Positive proof of identity including a recent photograph.

2. Either—

    (a) where the certificate is required for a purpose relating to section 115(5)(ea) of the Police Act 1997 (registration under Part II of the 2000 Act)(**a**), or the position falls within section 115(3) of that Act(**b**), an enhanced criminal record certificate issued under section 115 of that Act; or

    (b) in any other case, a criminal record certificate issued under sections 113 of that Act,

    including, where applicable, the matters specified in sections 113(3A) or 115(6A) of that Act(**c**).

3. Two written references, including a reference from the person's most recent employer, if any.

4. Where a person has previously worked in a position whose duties involved work with children or vulnerable adults, so far as reasonably practicable verification of the reason why the employment or position ended.

5. Documentary evidence of any relevant qualification.

6. A full employment history, together with a satisfactory written explanation of any gaps in employment.

7. Details of any criminal offences—

    (a) of which the person has been convicted, including details of any convictions which are spent within the meaning of section 1 of the Rehabilitation of Offenders Act 1974(**d**) and which may be disclosed by virtue of the Rehabilitation of Offenders Act 1974 (Exceptions) Order 1975(**e**); or

    (b) in respect of which he has been cautioned by a constable and which, at the time the caution was given, he admitted.

SCHEDULE 2   Regulation 22

RECORDS TO BE KEPT BY FOSTERING SERVICE PROVIDERS

1. A record in the form of a register showing in respect of each child placed with foster parents—

    (a) the date of his placement;

    (b) the name and address of the foster parent;

    (c) the date on which he ceased to be placed there;

    (d) his address prior to the placement;

    (e) his address on leaving the placement;

    (f) his responsible authority (if it is not the fostering service provider);

    (g) the statutory provision under which he is placed with foster parents.

2. A record showing in respect of each person working for the fostering service provider—

    (a) his full name;

    (b) his sex;

    (c) his date of birth;

    (d) his home address;

(**a**) 1997 c. 50 section 115(5)(ea) is inserted by the Care Standards Act 2000, section 104 on a date to be appointed. Sections 113 and 115, as amended, have not yet been brought into force.

(**b**) A position is within section 115(3) if it involves regularly caring for, training, supervising or being in sole charge of persons aged under 18.

(**c**) Sections 113(3A) and 115(6A) are added to the Police Act 1997 by section 8 of the Protection of Children Act 1999 (c. 14) on a date to be appointed, and amended by sections 104 and 116 of, and paragraph 25 of Schedule 4 to, the Care Standards Act 2000.

(**d**) 1974 c. 53.

(**e**) S.I. 1975/1023. Relevant amendments have been made by S.I. 1986/1249, S.I. 1986/2268 and S.I. 2001/1192.

(e) his qualifications relevant to, and experience of, work involving children;

(f) whether he is employed by the fostering service provider under a contract of service or a contract for services, or is employed by someone other than the fostering service provider;

(g) whether he works full-time or part-time and, if part-time, the average number of hours worked per week.

3. A record of all accidents occurring to children whilst placed with foster parents.

SCHEDULE 3   Regulation 27

INFORMATION AS TO PROSPECTIVE FOSTER PARENT AND OTHER MEMBERS OF HIS HOUSEHOLD AND FAMILY

1. His full name, address and date of birth.

2. Details of his health (supported by a medical report), personality, marital status and details of his current and any previous marriage or similar relationship.

3. Particulars of any other adult members of his household.

4. Particulars of the children in his family, whether or not members of his household, and any other children in his household.

5. Particulars of his accommodation.

6. His religious persuasion, and his capacity to care for a child from any particular religious persuasion.

7. His racial origin, his cultural and linguistic background and his capacity to care for a child from any particular origin or cultural or linguistic background.

8. His past and present employment or occupation, his standard of living and leisure activities and interests.

9. His previous experience (if any) of caring for his own and other children.

10. His skills, competence and potential relevant to his capacity to care effectively for a child placed with him.

11. The outcome of any request or application made by him or any other member of his household to foster or adopt children, or for registration for child minding or day care(**a**), including particulars of any previous approval or refusal of approval relating to him or to any other member of his household.

12. The names and addresses of two persons who will provide personal references for the prospective foster parent.

13. In relation to the prospective foster parent, either—

    (a) an enhanced criminal record certificate issued under section 115 of the Police Act 1997(**b**) including the matters specified in section 115(6A) of that Act; or

    (b) where any certificate of information on any matters referred to in sub-paragraph (a) is not available to an individual because any provision of the Police Act 1997 has not been brought into force, details of any criminal offences—

        (i) of which the person has been convicted, including details of any convictions which are spent within the meaning of section 1 of the Rehabilitation of Offenders Act 1974(**c**) and which may be disclosed by virtue of the Rehabilitation of Offenders Act 1974 (Exceptions) Order 1975(**d**); or

        (ii) in respect of which he has been cautioned by a constable and which, at the time the caution was given, he admitted; and

in relation to each member of the household aged 18 or over, details of any criminal offences such as are mentioned in sub-paragraphs (i) and (ii) of paragraph 13(b).

(**a**) Registration for child minding or day care is provided for by Part XA of the 1989 Act in respect of England and Wales and Part X of that Act in respect of Scotland.

(**b**) *See* the footnotes to paragraph 2 of Schedule 1.

(**c**) 1974 c. 53.

(**d**) S.I. 1975/1023. Relevant amendments have been made by S.I. 1986/1249, S.I. 1986/2268 and S.I. 2001/1192.

SCHEDULE 4   Regulation 27(7)(b)

OFFENCES SPECIFIED FOR THE PURPOSES OF REGULATION 27(7)(b)

Offences in Scotland

1. An offence of rape.

2. An offence specified in Schedule 1 to the Criminal Procedure (Scotland) Act 1995(**a**) except, in a case where the offender was under the age of 20 at the time the offence was committed, an offence contrary to section 5 of the Criminal Law (Consolidation) (Scotland) Act 1995 (intercourse with a girl under 16)(**b**), an offence of shameless indecency between men or an offence of sodomy.

3. An offence of plagium (theft of a child below the age of puberty).

4. Section 52 or 52A of the Civic Government (Scotland) Act 1982 (indecent photographs of children)(**c**).

5. An offence under section 3 of the Sexual Offences (Amendment) Act 2000 (abuse of trust)(**d**).

Offences in Northern Ireland

6. An offence of rape.

7. An offence specified in Schedule 1 to the Children and Young Persons Act (Northern Ireland) 1968(**e**), except in the case where the offender was under the age of 20 at the time the offence was committed, an offence contrary to sections 5 or 11 of the Criminal Law Amendment Act 1885 (unlawful carnal knowledge of a girl under 17 and gross indecency between males)(**f**), or an offence contrary to section 61 of the Offences against the Person Act 1861 (buggery).

8. An offence under Article 3 of the Protection of Children (Northern Ireland) Order 1978 (indecent photographs)(**g**).

9. An offence contrary to Article 9 of the Criminal Justice (Northern Ireland) Order 1980 (inciting girl under 16 to have incestuous sexual intercourse)(**h**).

10. An offence contrary to Article 15 of the Criminal Justice (Evidence, etc.) (Northern Ireland) Order 1988 (possession of indecent photographs of children)(**i**).

11. An offence under section 3 of the Sexual Offences (Amendment) Act 2000 (abuse of trust).

SCHEDULE 5   Regulation 28(5)(b)

MATTERS AND OBLIGATIONS IN FOSTER CARE AGREEMENTS

1. The terms of the foster parent's approval.

2. The amount of support and training to be given to the foster parent.

3. The procedure for the review of approval of a foster parent.

4. The procedure in connection with the placement of children and the matters to be included in any foster placement agreement.

5. The arrangements for meeting any legal liabilities of the foster parent arising by reason of a placement.

6. The procedure available to foster parents for making representations.

7. To give written notice to the fostering service provider forthwith, with full particulars, of—

(**a**) 1995 c. 46.
(**b**) 1995 c. 39.
(**c**) 1982 c. 45. Section 52A was inserted by section 161 of the Criminal Justice Act 1988(c. 33).
(**d**) 2000 c. 44.
(**e**) 1968 c. 34 (N.I.)
(**f**) 1885 c. 69.
(**g**) S.I. 1978/1047 (N.I.17).
(**h**) S.I. 1980/704 (N.I.6).
(**i**) S.I. 1988/1847 (N.I. 17).

(a) any intended change of the foster parent's address;

(b) any change in the composition of his household;

(c) any other change in his personal circumstances and any other event affecting either his capacity to care for any child placed or the suitability of his household; and

(d) any request or application to adopt children, or for registration for child minding or day care.

8. Not to administer corporal punishment to any child placed with him.

9. To ensure that any information relating to a child placed with him, to the child's family or to any other person, which has been given to him in confidence in connection with a placement is kept confidential and is not disclosed to any person without the consent of the fostering service provider.

10. To comply with the terms of any foster placement agreement.

11. To care for any child placed with him as if the child were a member of the foster parent's family and to promote his welfare having regard to the long and short-term plans for the child.

12. To comply with the policies and procedures of the fostering service provider issued under regulations 12 and 13.

13. To co-operate as reasonably required with the Commission and in particular to allow a person authorised by the Commission to interview him and visit his home at any reasonable time.

14. To keep the fostering service provider informed about the child's progress and to notify it immediately of any significant events affecting the child.

15. To allow any child placed with him to be removed from his home if regulation 36 applies.

SCHEDULE 6   Regulation 34(3)

MATTERS AND OBLIGATIONS IN FOSTER PLACEMENT AGREEMENTS

1. A statement by the responsible authority containing all the information which the authority considers necessary to enable the foster parent to care for the child and, in particular, information as to—

(a) the authority's arrangements for the child and the objectives of the placement in the context of its plan for the care of the child;

(b) the child's personal history, religious persuasion and cultural and linguistic background and racial origin;

(c) the child's state of health and identified health needs;

(d) the safety needs of the child, including any need for any special equipment or adaptation;

(e) the child's educational needs; and

(f) any needs arising from any disability the child may have.

2. The responsible authority's arrangements for the financial support of the child during the placement.

3. The arrangements for giving consent to the medical or dental examination or treatment of the child.

4. The circumstances in which it is necessary to obtain in advance the approval of the responsible authority for the child to take part in school trips, or to stay overnight away from the foster parent's home.

5. The arrangements for visits to the child by the person authorised by or on behalf of the responsible authority, and the frequency of visits and reviews under the Review of Children's Cases Regulations 1991(a).

6. The arrangements for the child to have contact with his parents and any other specified persons, and details of any court order relating to contact.

(a) S.I. 1991 No. 895 as amended by S.I. 1991 No. 2033, S.I. 1993 No. 3069, S.I. 1995 No. 2015 and S.I. 1997 No. 649.

7. Compliance by the foster parent with the terms of the foster care agreement.

8. Co-operation by the foster parent with the responsible authority regarding any arrangements it makes for the child.

SCHEDULE 7

Regulation 42(1)

MATTERS TO BE MONITORIED BY THE REGISTERED PERSON

1. Compliance in relation to each child placed with foster parents, with the foster placement agreement and the responsible authority's plan for the care of the child.

2. All accidents, injuries and illnesses of children placed with foster parents.

3. Complaints in relation to children placed with foster parents and their outcomes.

4. Any allegations or suspicions of abuse in respect of children placed with foster parents and the outcome of any investigation.

5. Recruitment records and conduct of required checks of new workers.

6. Notifications of events listed in Schedule 8.

7. Any unauthorised absence from the foster home of a child accommodated there.

8. Use of any measures of control, restraint or discipline in respect of children accommodated in a foster home.

9. Medication, medical treatment and first aid administered to any child placed with foster parents.

10. Where applicable, the standard of any education provided by the fostering service.

11. Records of assessments.

12. Records of fostering panel meetings.

13. Duty rosters of persons working for the fostering agency, as arranged and as actually worked.

14. Records of appraisals of employees.

15. Minutes of staff meetings.

SCHEDULE 8   Regulation 43(1)

EVENTS AND NOTIFICATIONS

Column 1 Event:	Column 2 To be notified to:					
	Commission	Responsible authority	Secretary of State	Area authority	Police	Health Authority
Death of a child placed with foster parents	yes	yes	yes	yes		yes
Referral to the Secretary of State pursuant to section 2(1)(a) of the Protection of Children Act 1999(**a**) of an individual working for a fostering service	yes	yes				
Serious illness or serious accident of a child placed with foster parents	yes	yes				
Outbreak at the home of a foster parent of any infectious disease which in the opinion of a registered medical practitioner attending the home is sufficiently serious to be so notified	yes	yes				yes
Allegation that a child placed with foster parents has committed a serious offence		yes			yes	
Involvement or suspected involvement of a child placed with foster parents in prostitution	yes	yes		yes	yes	
Serious incident relating to a child placed with foster parents necessitating calling the police to the foster parent's home	yes	yes				
Absconding by a child placed with foster parents		yes				
Any serious complaint about any foster parent approved by the fostering agency	yes	yes				
Instigation and outcome of any child protection enquiry involving a child placed with foster parents	yes	yes				

EXPLANATORY NOTE

(This note is not part of the Regulations)

These Regulations are made under the Children Act 1989 ("the 1989 Act") and the Care Standards Act 2000 ("the 2000 Act") and apply to England only. They—

    (a) replace the Foster Placement (Children) Regulations 1991 (as amended), governing the approval of foster parents and the placement of children with them by local authorities and voluntary organisations under, respectively, Parts III and VII of the 1989 Act; and

    (b) provide a new regulatory framework for fostering agencies and local authority fostering services.

By section 4(4) of the 2000 Act, "fostering agency" means either an undertaking which discharges functions of local authorities in connection with the placing of children with foster parents (in these Regulations called "an independent fostering agency"), or a voluntary organisation which places children with foster parents under section 59(1) of the Children Act (an agency within the meaning of section 4(4)(b)). An independent fostering agency may, but need not, be carried on by a voluntary organisation, and if so, it may in some cases, also be an agency within the meaning of section 4(4)(b).

Part II of the 2000 Act provides for the registration and inspection of establishments and agencies, including fostering agencies, by the National Care Standards Commission ("the Commission"). Part III of the 2000 Act provides for the inspection of the fostering functions of local authorities by the Commission. These will not be registered, but the Act provides for failings to be reported to the Secretary of State. Parts II and III of the 2000 Act (so far as not already in force) will be brought into force in relation to fostering agencies and local authority fostering services on 1st April 2002.

These Regulations are intended to establish, so far as possible, a common framework for fostering services, whether provided by local authorities, voluntary organisations, or independent fostering agencies acting under delegation arrangements ("fostering services").

By regulation 3, each fostering service must have a statement of purpose setting out the aims and objectives of the service and the facilities and services to be provided, and a children's guide. The fostering service must be carried on in a manner which is consistent with the statement of purpose.

Regulations 5 to 10 make provision about the persons carrying on and managing the fostering service, and require a manager to be appointed for the service (regulations 6 and 10). The fitness of the provider of a fostering agency and of the manager of a fostering service is provided for, in particular by reference to the matters prescribed in Schedule 1. Where the provider of a fostering agency is an organisation, it must nominate a responsible individual who must satisfy the requirements as to fitness. Regulation 8 imposes general requirements in relation to the proper conduct of a fostering service, and as to training.

Part III makes provision about the conduct of a fostering service, in particular, as to child protection, behaviour, contact, health and education, and support for foster parents. Provision is also made about the staffing of fostering services, the fitness of workers and premises, and record keeping. Provision is made as to the promotion of child welfare by, and complaints in respect of, independent fostering agencies (regulations 11 and 18).

Part IV deals with the approval of foster parents by fostering services. It requires a fostering panel to be established in respect of each fostering service (regulations 24 to 26). Regulation 27 sets out the procedure for the assessment of persons wishing to become foster parents, and makes provision as to the circumstances in which persons may not be considered suitable to act as foster parents. Regulations 28 and 29 provide for the approval, review of approval and termination of approval of foster parents. Regulations 30 to 32 provide for records and a register to be kept.

Part V deals with the placement of children with foster parents by local authorities and voluntary organisations ("responsible authorities"). Regulations 33 to 36 impose general requirements on responsible authorities as to the making, supervision and termination of placements, and regulations 37 and 38 make specific provision about short-term placements, and emergency and immediate placements by local authorities. Relations between a local authority and an independent fostering agency are governed by regulation 40.

Part VI (regulation 41) provides for visits to be made by an officer of the local authority to children who are placed with foster parents by voluntary organisations (section 62 of the 1989 Act).

Part VII makes miscellaneous provision regarding fostering agencies. The registered person is required to monitor the matters set out in Schedule 7 relating to the quality of care provided (regulation 42), and to give notice of the events listed in Schedule 8 to the persons mentioned in that Schedule (regulation 43). Regulation 44 imposes requirements relating to the agency's financial position. Regulations 45 to 47 provide for the giving of notices to the Commission and the appointment of liquidators.

Regulation 48 provides for offences in relation to fostering agencies. A breach of the regulations specified in regulation 48(1) may found an offence on the part of the registered person. However, no prosecution may be brought unless the Commission has first given the registered person a notice which sets out in what respect it is alleged he is not complying with a regulation, and what action the Commission considers it is necessary for him to take in order to comply. The notice must specify a time period for compliance, not exceeding three months.

Regulation 50 makes transitional provision. These Regulations apply to local authority fostering services on their coming into force. By regulation 50 (1) and (2) they will also apply to a voluntary organisation which places children with foster parents under section 59 of the 1989 Act, which has duly applied to the Commission for registration as a fostering agency by 1st April 2002. These Regulations do not apply to an independent fostering agency until it is registered, but sub-paragraphs (3) to (5) of this regulation allow a local authority to delegate certain duties to an independent fostering agency which has by 1st April 2002 applied to the Commission for registration. Regulation 50(7) disapplies regulation 20(6) (which limits the circumstances in which a person who is approved as a foster parent by a fostering service may also be employed to work for the purposes of the service), in certain cases.